landscaping with
stone

CRE**A**TIVE
HOMEOWNER®

landscaping with
stone

PAT SAGUI

CREATIVE HOMEOWNER®, Upper Saddle River, New Jersey

VP/Editorial Director: Timothy O. Bakke
Production Managers: Kimberly H. Vivas,
   Rose Sullivan

Senior Editor: Fran J. Donegan
Photo Researchers: Lauren Manoy, Jennifer Ramcke
Editorial Assistant: Evan Lambert
Indexer: Schroeder Indexing Services

Design and Layout: David Geer
Illustrations: Elayne Sears, Michele Angle Farrar,
   Robert LaPointe
Front Cover Photography: (top to bottom, left to right) Walter Chandoha; Brian Vanden Brink; John Glover; Garden Picture Library/John Beedle; Todd Caverly/Brian Vanden Brink Photos
Back Cover Photography: (top) Gay Bumgarner; (center) Karen Bussolini

Manufactured in the United States of America

Current Printing (last digit)
10 9 8 7 6

Landscaping with Stone, First Edition
Library of Congress Control Number: 2004103762
ISBN: 1-58011-112-2

CREATIVE HOMEOWNER®
A Division of Federal Marketing Corp.
24 Park Way, Upper Saddle River, NJ 07458
www.creativehomeowner.com

Safety First

All projects and procedures in this book have been reviewed for safety; still it is not possible to overstate the importance of working carefully. What follows are reminders for plant care and project safety. Always use common sense.

- *Always* use caution, care, and good judgment when following the procedures in this book.
- *Always* determine locations of underground utility lines before you dig, and then avoid them by a safe distance. Buried lines may be for gas, electricity, communications, or water. Contact local utility companies who will help you map their lines.
- *Always* read and heed tool manufacturer instructions.
- *Always* ensure that the electrical setup is safe; be sure that no circuit is overloaded and that all power tools and electrical outlets are properly grounded and protected by a ground-fault circuit interrupter (GCFI). Do not use power tools in wet locations.
- *Always* wear eye protection when using chemicals, sawing wood, pruning trees and shrubs, using power tools, and striking metal onto metal or concrete.
- *Always* consider nontoxic and least toxic methods of addressing unwanted plants, plant pests, and plant diseases before resorting to toxic methods. Follow package application and safety instructions carefully.
- *Always* read labels on chemicals, solvents, and other products; provide ventilation; heed warnings.
- *Always* wear a hard hat when working in situations with potential for injury from falling tree limbs.
- *Always* wear appropriate gloves in situations in which your hands could be injured by rough surfaces, sharp edges, thorns, or poisonous plants.
- *Always* protect yourself against ticks, which can carry Lyme disease. Wear light-colored, long-sleeved shirts and pants. Inspect yourself for ticks after every session in the garden.
- *Always* wear a disposable face mask or a special filtering respirator when creating sawdust or working with toxic gardening substances.
- *Always* keep your hands and other body parts away from the business end of blades, cutters, and bits.
- *Always* obtain approval from local building officials before undertaking construction of permanent structures.
- *Never* employ herbicides, pesticides, or toxic chemicals unless you have determined with certainty that they were developed for the specific problem you hope to remedy.
- *Never* allow bystanders to approach work areas where they might by injured by workers or work site hazards.
- *Never* work with power tools when you are tired, or under the influence of alcohol or drugs.
- *Never* carry sharp or pointed tools, such as knives or saws, in your pocket.

Acknowledgments

Masons, landscape architects, designers, sculptors and homeowners graciously contributed projects and their hard-earned experience to this book. I am deeply indebted and grateful to them, especially to the following for their generosity and kindness in the form of advice, projects, and suggestions. Great thanks to you, Andrea Morgante, Charlie Proutt, Peter Morris, Catherine Clemens, Mark Shorey, David Newton, Paul Wieczoreck, Justin Rose, Stony Mason, Wes Patnaude, Miriam Klein, Bill Henchey, Michael Lawrence, Bill Hayes, Mick O'Neill, Bo Bergstrom, John Doane, Bruce Culver, Dave Brett, Kevin Baker, Charlie McClintock, photographer Carolyn Bates, and the Chicago Botanical Garden. I am also indebted to the landscape architects and educators whose books inspired and helped me distill a vast body of know-how into a "how-to" primer. To the editor of record, Fran Donegan, who came on the scene after the manuscript was complete, my sincere appreciation for his patience with a first-time author. Special thanks to Charlie Proutt and Danny Young for reading the manuscript and making suggestions to improve it; to Miranda Smith for her tutelage; and to Brian and Will for their good humor and understanding, without which I could not take on projects that add unimagined wanderings to our life.

Contents

Introduction

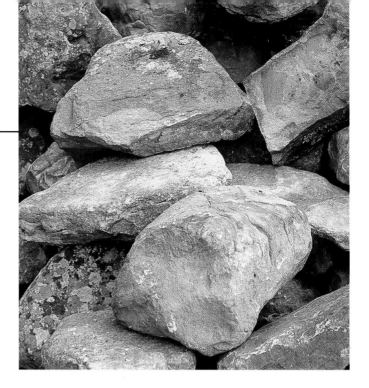

This book is for the homeowner who wants to include natural stone in his or her landscape design. More than ever before, the availability of different types of stone and the ease of renting stone-moving equipment make ambitious projects possible—even for homeowners who have no experience working with stone as a landscaping material.

Stone can be used to great effect in all landscapes. For thousands of years it has served our needs and our fancy. Craftsmen have quarried, hauled, stacked, shaped, laid, mortared, set, shimmed, and carved stone with a breadth of craft and ingenuity that is both awe inspiring and humbling. Those projects are an inspiration to all homeowners who want to include stonework in their designs.

Above: The availability of stone-moving equipment makes large projects possible.

Below: Stone is a popular material for patios, walls, and landscape steps.

Opposite: A dry-laid stone wall is used as a divider and as a planter for bulbs and perennials.

Good stonework takes both physical and creative energy. It also takes the skills and procedures common to all successful projects: realistic expectations, reliable suppliers and subcontractors, good record keeping, patience, and an appreciation for sweat equity. At roughly 160 pounds to the cubic foot, stonework will test your mettle.

Landscaping with Stone can take the guesswork out of your project. Use the information to complete a project on your own, or rely on it for guidance when collaborating with a mason or designer.

Design and Planning

The first four chapters help you think of stone as a landscaping element. Use them to guide you through defining the overall style of a project, evaluating the site, choosing the stone, and coordinating an installation. A chapter on tools and techniques will introduce you to some of the tools that could make your project go more smoothly. The plan presented in these chapters helps you stay organized, keep your momentum, and make the best use of your resources.

Stone Projects

Chapters 5 through 12 each look at a specific stonework project. These chapters feature the voices of experience—homeowners, designers, landscapers, and masons who generously contributed information for this book. Their projects are from geographic areas of the U.S. where natural stone is plentiful and there is a tradition of using stone in gardens and landscapes. Each chapter includes design information, dozens of photographs of stonework projects, and installation guidance.

Below: Using native stone adds an organic element to your landscape design.

Opposite top: Stone projects can have both functional and sculptural qualities.

Opposite bottom: Stone works well with plants, water, and other garden features.

Why Do Stonework?

Each of us has our own reasons for choosing to participate in do-it-yourself projects. Financial incentives, the pleasure of physical work, the joy of learning, and creative stimulation are all familiar reasons to do-it-yourselfers. If you possess one or more of these inclinations, you can complete a landscaping project using stone. Technical and expressive abilities are important, but more than anything else, success hinges on your mental and physical investment in the project.

Use *Landscaping with Stone* to help you add natural beauty and value to your property. It is packed with the inspiration and technical know-how that will help you transform rough sketches and inspired daydreams into your own designs and completed stonework projects.

CHAPTER 1

Designing with
Stone

Stone may be the most versatile land-scape building material available. Its qualities of strength and durability make it an excellent choice for garden paths, patios, and walls. But the decorative side of stone provides those landscape elements with a unique sense of style and makes stone a good choice for water features, rock gardens, and well-placed groupings that mimic nature or sculpture. This chapter will show you how to incorporate stone into your landscape design.

Decide What You Like

As you begin to plan your own project, you will need to make some decisions about the scope and elements in the project. What type of project are you planning? What are its proposed dimensions? What types of stone will you use for the project? Who will do the work?

Studying examples of existing stonework in walls, patios, and other landscape features is one of the best ways to begin to discover your preferences for stonework details. Stone found in nature, a neighbor's yard, the local botanical garden, and everything in between are places where you can see how stone is used. Not only can you learn what is possible from these examples, you can also discover what you like.

Explore the Possibilities

When trying to incorporate a new patio into your yard, add a rustic-looking stone wall to the garden, or build any stone-based project, rely on basic design principles to help the project best fit in with its surroundings.

Scale and Proportion. The scale and proportion of an object work hand in hand. The scale of something refers to its size as it relates to everything else. A 10-foot-high stone wall will tower over everything in the yard, including the people who use the space. It may be a good choice if you want total privacy and

Below: When laying out a new patio, remember that it will look best if it is kept in proportion to the surroundings.

Gathering Information for Your Project

- Bring home samples from quarries or masonry supply yards.
- Mark examples in books and magazines that you like, both whole landscapes and specific elements.
- Take photos of constructed and natural landscapes, and stonework that appeal to you.
- Take measurements and make notes to go with photos: location, type of stone, contact person, and so on.
- Notice how different path materials feel underfoot and how they affect your walking pace.
- View the most appealing projects and natural settings in all seasons.
- View projects in the dark with artificial light if you'll use the area in the evening.

security, but a 3-foot-high wall may make more sense if you simply want to define an herb garden.

Proportion refers to the relationship of objects to one another based on size—the size of the patio is in proportion to the size of the yard. Good scale is achieved when all of the parts complement one another proportionally.

Line. Simply put, lines define space, but they also suggest various qualities. A straight line implies strength and formality: a straight path almost always appears formal. A curving, winding path denotes a certain freedom and casualness.

Balance. In a landscape, balance refers to the effects created by the mix of elements you use. The features of a landscape are in balance when they look as though they belong together and the arrangement is pleasing to the eye. Balanced relationships can be either symmetrical or asymmetrical.

Above: These large slab steps are balanced by the massive stones flanking the stair.

Left: Repeating patterns create a rhythm in your design that is pleasing to the eye.

Design Tip

Find Inspiration Everywhere

Check garden and home decorating magazines for stonework ideas; ask to see the portfolios of designers or masons; and go on tours of local gardens. To find local garden tours, check with local garden clubs and the Garden Conservancy's Open Days Directory. (Call 845-265-2029 or click on www.garden-conservancy.org for more information.)

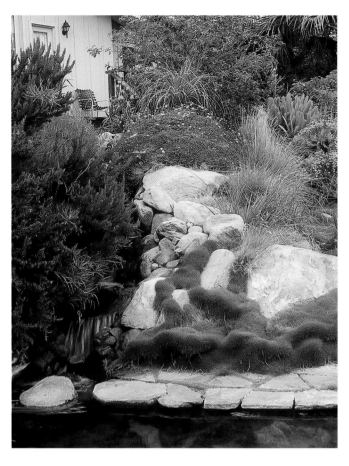

Harmony and Rhythm. In a harmonious plan, all of the elements share characteristics such as size, shape, or color. An example would be a patio and wall that are made from the same type stone. Rhythm refers to repeated patterns. When you vary one or more of the above traits in a repetitive pattern, it creates a visual rhythm. The key to creating good harmony and rhythm is balance.

Texture and Color. Stone is available in a variety of colors and textures. As you begin to design your project, you'll discover that stone can convey almost any feeling you want—grandeur, elegance, simplicity, solitude, durability, utility, and order are all possible. Stone can even suggest something other than what is. A dry streambed is a classic example of this.

Above: Stones of various sizes alter the texture of this lush hillside.

Below: Create visual interest by combining stonework with well-placed plantings.

Popular Stonework Projects

Stonework for gardens and landscapes generally fits into one of three categories: it imitates nature; it's functional; or it's sculptural. Some projects combine categories or serve multiple functions. Here are some additional stonework projects.

Stonework that Imitates Nature
- Ponds
- Streams and dry stream beds
- Waterfalls
- Rocky outcroppings
- Scree
- Boulders set in beds, open spaces, or woods
- Stepping-stones over water

Functional Stonework
- Stepping-stones
- Firepits and fireplaces
- Pool surrounds and copings
- Erosion control
- Seating and tables
- Edgings
- Terraces
- Grade changes
- Lanterns
- Containers for plants
- Bridges

Sculptural Stonework
- Specimen stones, one or a group
- Waterbowls
- Birdbaths
- Carved or cast figurative and abstract pieces
- Relief carvings
- Mosaics
- Objects in stone or other materials incorporated into stonework

Above right: This unusual spiral design moves the eye to the center of the patio and then to the patio's edge.

Right: Using similar stones of varied size and shape leads to a pleasing overall design.

DESIGNING WITH STONE

1

Aesthetic Decisions for Stonework

When you work with stone, you make decisions about the qualities of the stone you use, the quantities or distribution of the stone, and the way that the project transitions to its surroundings. For flat work such as patios and walkways, you also have to make choices about bedding—how the stone is set in place. The decisions you make about each of these factors will affect the overall look of your project and how well it is integrated into the site.

The Physical Qualities of Stone. The physical qualities of stone can contribute varying degrees of formality to a project. Variations in color and composition, the texture of exposed faces, fracture lines, and the size and shape of individual stones contribute to the distinctive character of each stone type.

Smooth surfaces are more formal that rough ones, large uniformly shaped pieces are more formal than irregular smaller pieces. For example, if you build a patio using 2-foot-square pieces of sawn bluestone set with ¼-inch joints, it will be more formal or conservative than if you had used irregular shaped pieces of a stone with more varied color and with a rough or cleaved surface. (See "Choosing Between Formal and Informal Designs," page 21.)

The Quantity or Distribution of Stone. Quantity or distribution refers to how much stone you use and how you arrange and space the stone. Distribution includes the relationship between stones in a grouping of stones, the ratio of stone to vegetation, and the way you combine different types of stone. In both walls and flat work, stones fitted tightly together create a more formal project than those with irregular or larger joints. In some projects, it's important to consider the amount of stone that will be hidden as vegetation matures. With foresight, you can create different effects by using seasonal changes. A hillside rock garden can be a riot of cultivated color in summer, for example, but can change to a wild, rugged place in winter.

Distribution is perhaps most critical when you make an artful arrangement of large stones. The stones must have sufficient proximity to create a composition but be far enough from one another that each makes a distinct contribution to the overall arrangement.

Above: The sizes and shapes of these stones contribute to the informal look of this wall.

Opposite: Stone projects range from the simple to the truly ornate as shown here.

Transitions. It can be challenging to figure out how to transition from your stonework to the surrounding area, such as to lawn or a driveway. Fortunately there are many options from which to choose. If you're not sure what will work best, try experimenting with different treatments in a small area to evaluate possible solutions. Ground covers, timbers, bark mulch, gravel, a grade change, and hedging are common transitioning solutions. You can even plant one or more shrubs to hide a difficult transition for which you can't find another solution. Transitions around a patio are relatively easy and straightforward. Fencing, flowerbeds, hedging, or a stone wall are all commonly used.

It's easy and tempting to ignore transitions until after the main elements of a project are installed. Don't! Careless transitions detract from your project and may forever look like an afterthought.

Below: Although distinct from the plantings, this gravel walk appears to blend into the surrounding vegetation.

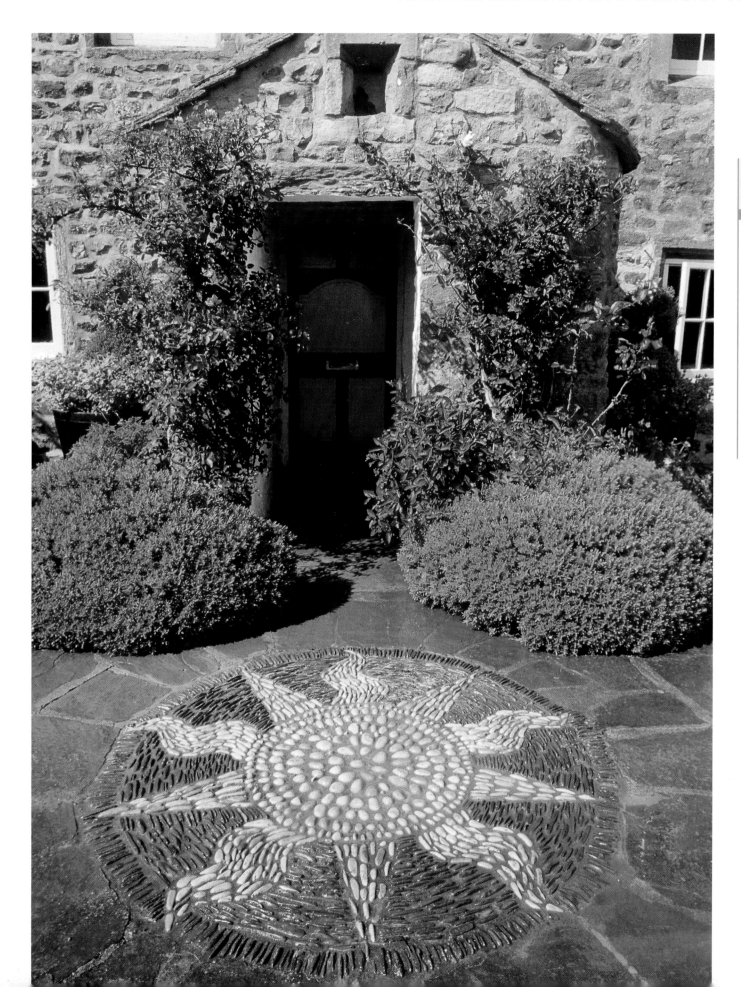

Smart Tip

Don't Forget about Future Maintenance

When making decisions about bedding for flat work, think about maintenance. Mortared joints require the least amount of maintenance, though they do eventually crumble. Sand-filled joints need to be refilled periodically. Planted and sand-filled joints require occasional weeding from blown-in seed.

Below: In general, dry-laid patios or walls appear more informal than a structure installed with mortar-filled joints.

Bedding Choices. Stone is either dry laid or mortared in place. With either option, bedding variables affect the appearance of the stonework. Variables include the size of the joints, or spaces between stones, whether the spaces are filled in, and the fill material. As a general rule, mortared, uniform, narrow joints are the most formal. Going back to the patio example, if your joints are irregular and large enough for planting a ground cover, the effect will be more casual than if the joints are uniform and filled with sand. Again, experiment with different possibilities. Notice the choices that designers have made in similar projects. Observations like these help inform your decisions.

Choosing between Formal and Informal Designs

The type of stone you select and its distribution, transitions, and bedding will influence the look and formality of your project. Here are some elements to consider.

Formal Designs	Informal Designs
smooth surface	rough or irregular surface
cut or sawn stone	cleaved or weathered flat surface
uniform, rectangular shapes	irregular shapes
repetitive pattern	random or multiple patterns
uniform color	variations in color
homogeneous composition	nonhomogeneous composition
small joints	large joints (¾ in. or more)
uniform joints	irregular joint width
mortared joints	sand, gravel, soil with ground cover in joints
one type of stone	two or more types of stone
tall retainer walls	terraced retainer walls
uniform size and color of gravel	mixed gravel
large project (big patio, large water feature)	small-scale projects
edging materials	**edging materials**
square timbers	round timbers
brick or other uniformly shaped stones	random-size stones
gravel	bark mulch
formal flower beds	ground covers

DESIGNING WITH STONE

1

Developing a Design Direction

Have you collected numerous photos of stonework constructed with a particular kind of stone or pattern? Perhaps a particular color, texture, or shape of stone dominates your samples. It's a good indication that you're forming personal preferences about stonework when these decision-making patterns emerge.

Notice what is most outstanding about the projects you like. Sometimes it's not even the stone, but something adjacent to it, such as water or a specimen plant. Specific rather than general observations yield the most information and build confidence for your decisions about these details. Asking questions about existing projects helps you identify overlooked considerations, too.

Often ideas and features that continue to engage you end up influencing the look of your project. Or you may deliberately incorporate specific ideas or features you've discovered.

Another indicator of emerging preferences is your intuitive response to a type of stone or installation. Sometimes this is called comfort level. Whatever you call it, the experience is an overriding sense that the stone, pattern, type of installation, and so on, is right for you, right for the site, or would just work well.

Above right: When researching stone projects, look for examples where the stone complements the area.

Below: Sometimes a stone project is a good way to draw attention to a planting area.

Right: A colorful planted border flanks a mortared walkway of multicolored flagstones.

Analyze Your Research

As you look at completed stonework projects and natural landscapes that you like, ask the following:

- What do I like about the stone?
- How is the transition made from the stone to whatever adjoins or abuts it?
- Can I identify specific features or elements besides the stone that make this space pleasing to me?
- How do the shape, arrangement, texture, quantity, and types of stone contribute to the overall formality and effect?
- How would I describe the overall effect?
- How do I respond to the quality of "fullness" or "emptiness" in this installation?
- Does the stonework define or create space?
- Does the stonework create a microclimate by trapping heat or creating shade?
- How much stone is used?
- In the settings that you like the best, what percentage of the total project area is stone?
- How much stone is visible at different times of the year, i.e., with or without plants in leaf?

Above: Although the designer used two different types of stone, the wall and patio work well together as a design.

Left: Don't be afraid to juxtapose shapes and patterns to create a truly unique design.

Tradeoffs. Ultimately, there are tradeoffs between design goals, site possibilities, and the budget. Many homeowners find this part of the design process the hardest. In these cases, it is often best to seek out the opinions of friends and acquaintances. Eventually, you start to trust in the process, and an aesthetic emerges that works for you and the site.

Inspiration from the Site

The site for your project is a valuable source of inspiration. Often the land itself suggests use and design possibilities that can influence the overall project plan. Professional designers always consider a site's assets as part of the design phase of a project; this approach makes sense for homeowners as well. It's usually less expensive to work with, rather than alter, existing site conditions. It's also easier—and you're more likely—to end up with a project that is well integrated into its surroundings. You'll find more on working with the site in Chapter 2.

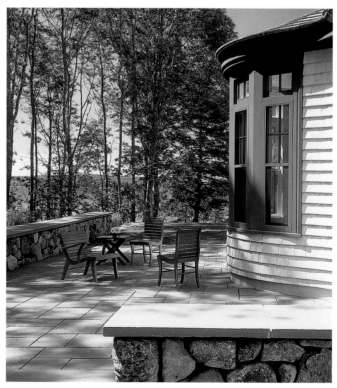

Above: When placing large stones, strive for a natural arrangement such as the one shown here.

Above right: A solid-looking stone wall appears to support the building constructed above it.

Right: Using natural materials always helps a design blend in with the surrounding area.

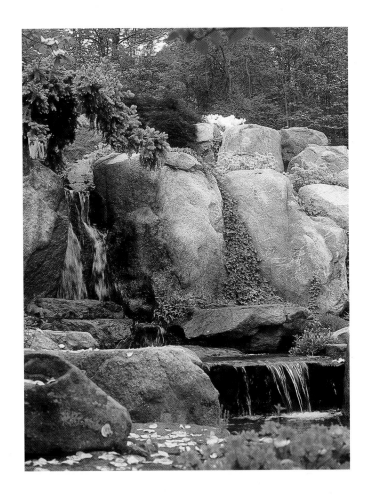

Use Props

Visual aids help you explore ideas and prepare for installing your project. Use cardboard cutouts to make path "stones" a pattern for a patio, or as a way to envision a retainer wall or steps. Use malleable materials such as chicken wire and crumpled-up paper to test the location of large boulders. Branches and small trees can represent future mature plants. Garden hose and rope work well to outline paths, beds, water features, or a patio. Even grade stakes and string are useful to help you visualize the space as you plan to reconfigure it.

Be Curious about Your Materials. Play with stone the way an artist experiments with materials. Explore and test patterns, spacing, and the effect of light and shade. Observe how different stones look and feel when they are wet. Study the relationship between stone and its surroundings in existing projects. These exercises provide a basis for decisions that will affect the look of your stonework.

Nature is your best teacher for stone projects that mimic natural features. If you plan a project such as a streambed or rocky wooded hillside, studying the way stone is naturally distributed in these settings can help you adapt desirable qualities to your site.

It takes effort to adapt your personal style to stonework. A spirit of adventure helps, too. But if you explore possibilities early on in a project, you'll find it easier to make design decisions. What you learn during the exploration process makes it possible to turn a pile of stone into something that pleases you.

1

DESIGNING WITH STONE

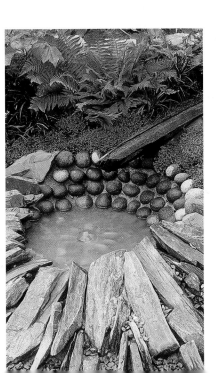

Above left: Water features like this are possible with professional help.

Far left: A backyard pond has an Asian theme.

Left: The designer used shards of stone to rim this small water feature.

Creating Walkways & Steps

In purely functional terms, steps, paths, walkways, and stepping-stones help you get from one part of the yard to another. But they also serve as a unifying element in the landscape design by providing your eye with a bridge that connects one design element or area with another. You can strengthen this connection by using walkways or steps to connect elements, such as two stone walls or a wall and patio, that are made from the same type stone. Tie the whole design together by using a similar stone for the walkway.

Left: The stones that edge this simple gravel path were found on the property and help tie the design to the site.

Above: Quarried slabs of stone serve as steps that wind up a steep incline.

Below left: The random pattern of this walkway creates an informal feeling for the area.

Below: Set walkways stones in sand as shown here or in mortar for a permanent installation.

Above: Adding steps and support walls on a hillside may require the expertise of a landscape professional.

More Walkways & Steps

Far left: Full-size treads are supported by smaller evenly cut stones.

Left: Large stepping-stones seem to float in a sea of smaller stones.

Above: Native stone easily blends with the surrounding area.

Below: A slight curve adds interest to any walkway.

Above: Combine different types of stone to create unique walkway patterns.

Below: For design continuity, the owner used the same stone on the steps and the retaining walls.

Above: In this shaded spot, stepping-stones complement rather than overwhelm the plantings in the area.

Below: Formal steps connect mortared patios. Note the stone seat built into the wall.

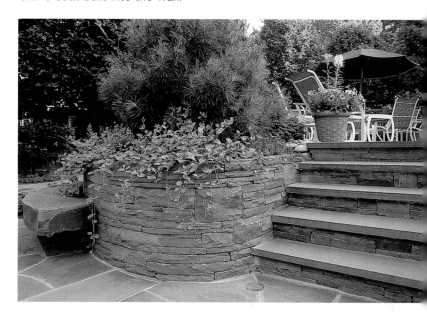

Creating Stone Patios

Patios add the natural structure found indoors to outdoor living spaces. They are destinations that people in the yard seek out and tend to gravitate toward. As with any interior living space, design patios so that they can accommodate any activities you plan for the area. Most people plan patios as spaces that allow them to sit and enjoy the scenery, but don't forget other possible uses, including areas to entertain, cooking spaces, and places that allow you to keep an eye on young children who want to play outside.

Below: Stone complements other materials, such as this wood fence, the furniture, and the brick wall.

Right: Well-designed stonework always looks as though it has always been part of the site.

Bottom: Classic-style columns and parts of columns give this unusual patio a formal feel.

Far left: Use loose gravel to carve out part of a yard for a seating area.

Left: A stone patio is the perfect location for a potting or hobby table.

Below: This patio looks almost too natural to have been built.

More Stone Patios

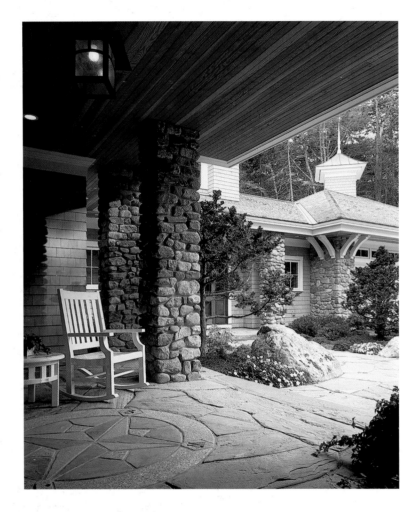

Left: Expert craftsman can create designs like this from native stone.

Above: This view shows what you can do when combining different materials in one design.

Below left: In many areas, native stone is the material of choice for outdoor living areas.

Below: A well-sited patio incorporates the view into the living space.

Opposite: This well-built wall defines the boundaries of the patio area.

More Stone Patios

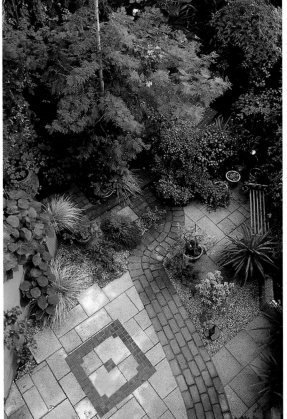

Left: Expert craftsman can create designs like this from native stone.

Above: This view shows what you can do when combining different materials in one design.

Below left: In many areas, native stone is the material of choice for outdoor living areas.

Below: A well-sited patio incorporates the view into the living space.

Opposite: This well-built wall defines the boundaries of the patio area.

Far left: Use loose gravel to carve out part of a yard for a seating area.

Left: A stone patio is the perfect location for a potting or hobby table.

Below: This patio looks almost too natural to have been built.

1

DESIGNING WITH STONE

Creating Walls

Walls form boundaries that separate your yard from your neighbor's or divide up your property into smaller sections. A stone retaining wall or a group of walls turns a sloping yard into level, usable areas. Stone walls also provide a feeling of stability and strength that few other landscape elements can. Stone walls are either dry laid or mortared in place. A dry-laid wall tends to be more casual than a mortared version, but the selection of stone and the design of the wall determine the look of the finished project.

Above: Stone walls impart a feeling of solidity to a landscape.

Top right: Create dry-laid retaining walls with field stones from your property.

Right: This bench stone extends back into the hillside for support.

Right: Ashlar is any stone cut into square or rectangular shapes.

Below: A mortared fieldstone wall serves as backdrop for flowering plants.

Below right: Unusual designs such as this are difficult to incorporate into the home landscape.

Bottom right: An informal wall borders a lush garden.

More Walls

Above: Both dry-laid and mortared stone walls rely on staggered joints for stability.

Below: While most stone walls run straight, the occasional curve adds design interest.

Above: Mortared walls are difficult to build, but they make unusual designs possible.

Below: A large arched alcove is the focal point of this retaining wall.

Above: High privacy walls are tricky to build and are best left to a qualified professional.

Creating Rock Features

Arock feature can be a rock garden, a grouping of stones that has the look of sculpture, a birdbath, dry creek bed, or any one of dozens of other designs. In fact, most large water features rely on stone to provide the borders for the feature, and in streams and waterfalls, stone often directs water flow. You can let your imagination and creativity run a little wild when designing a rock feature, but you must still take care in placing the stones and arranging them in a way that makes good design sense.

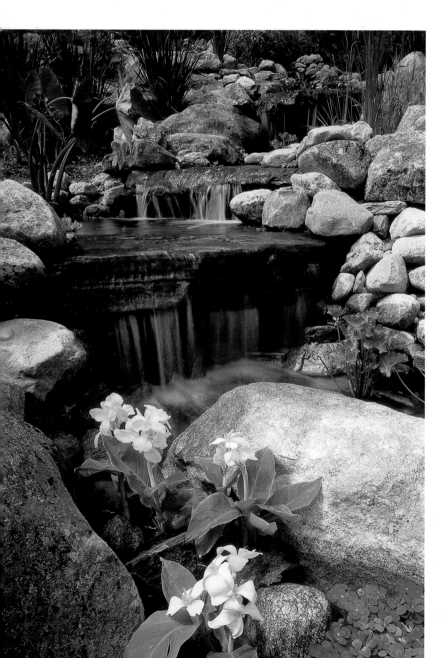

Left: This large water feature gets its natural look from the use of native stone.

Below: Plant retaining walls with hardy plants to create vertical rock gardens.

Bottom: Stone provides a site with authenticity, and it helps hide the edges of a pond liner.

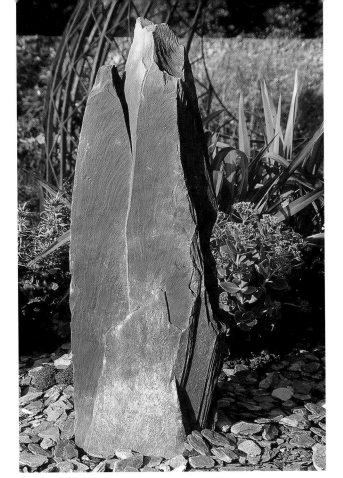

Stone as a Design Element

You can use stone to change the look and feel of a space. The size and shape of the stones, their color, quantity, spacing, and placement all contribute to the overall character of your project. Note these elements as you look at examples of stonework.

Far left: A well-placed stone resembles a piece of sculpture.

Left: River-washed stones complete a bubbling spring.

Below: With effort, stone can become a planter.

More Rock Features

Far left: Stones and raked sand are basic elements of Japanese gardens.

Left: Stones provide the backbone for this garden.

Below: Mixing materials creates visual excitement.

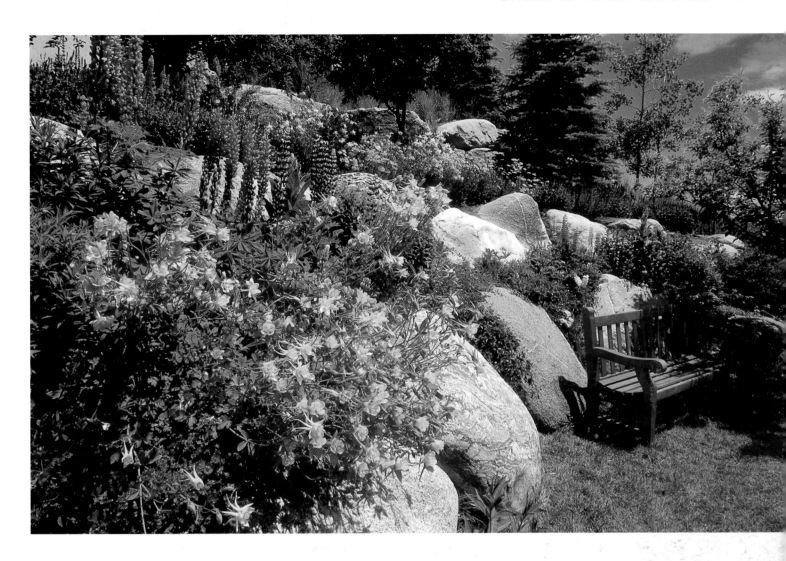

Above: There is an art to placing large stones in a landscape.

Right: The washed stones in the fountain draw the eye to the feature.

Below: Stones create a natural looking waterfall and pool.

CHAPTER 2

Planning Your
Project

Once you have a picture in your mind of the stonework project you want, it's time to take a long, hard look at the building site. You can make the best use of your site only when you have a thorough understanding of its limitations as well as its assets. Having a detailed overview or "big picture" is key to refining your project design. No detail is too small to be ignored when you are planning a stonework project—it's far easier to correct an error with your pencil than with your back.

Defining the Site

When creating a stonework project, the space you'll need always extends beyond its footprint. The site will include access areas for deliveries; storage areas for stone, backfill, or bedding material; storage for disturbed subsoil and topsoil that will be redistributed afterwards; a place to care for plants; underground utilities and drainage pipes; and buildings or parts of buildings that are essentially part of the site. For example, if you install a patio adjacent to one side of the house, that side of the house is part of the site, along with any windows, porches, or decks that offer views of the site.

Design Tip

Play with the Space

If possible, try to stage the planned changes and then live with the arrangement for a few weeks. For example, you can move chairs into various positions and sit in them to simulate a patio. Or use a garden hose to lay out a proposed walk. Most of us don't often get a chance to play with space, but this is an effective way to refine a plan.

Your site may also include locations for temporary dikes or ditches that prevent erosion during the installation. If your project involves the use of large equipment, the space needed to maneuver the equipment is also part of your site.

Be Neighborly. Sometimes a site limited to one property isn't big enough to manage a project efficiently. If this is your situation, consider asking an adjoining property owner for permission to use whatever additional space you need to handle materials efficiently. It may be a good idea to draw up a written agreement with the neighbor. Or look into using part of the street if possible.

Site Evaluation

Unlike the mental free rein you give yourself when exploring aesthetic choices, you need to be more deliberate with the site evaluation. It is literally an inventory of the items on your property. No detail is too small to ignore: identify all of the site's features, potential, and limits. Then transfer this information to plan and elevation drawings.

Below: The mundane work of site evaluation leads to beautiful results, such as this hillside garden.

Site Evaluation Checklist

Use this list to evaluate the site of the project. If a contractor or landscaping firm is doing the work, use this list to check its work.

Locate

Property lines

Rights-of-way (Check the property deed.)

Buried services (Maps are available from utility companies.)

Telecom cables

Water, gas, sewer, and electric lines

Drainage tile (Check with previous owner or the architect, or look for outlets in low spots.)

Identify

Soil type(s)

New permanent paths for foot and vehicle traffic

Topography to preserve or alter

Vegetation to preserve and store for reinstallation

Vegetation to protect from damage during installation

Vulnerable roots of large trees and plants

Microclimate possibilities

Water to incorporate into plan or divert

Stone to incorporate into plan or remove

New drainage requirements

Areas to light artificially and the kind of light desired

Airflow patterns to maintain or alter

Sun and shade to maintain or alter

Points of transition from existing to new features

Impact of new features on possible future building or landscaping plans

Zoning Restrictions and Permit Requirements (Check with municipal offices.)

Setback requirements

Permits

Erosion control (large projects)

Site Management Requirements

Access for deliveries

Physical space to unload

Adequate ground conditions to support loaded vehicles

Travel paths for construction-related activities

Storage space for stone, base or bedding material; excavated topsoil and subsoil; plants

Boundary of excavated area

Off-site disposal of excess excavated soil

Space to maneuver equipment

Flags or ropes to delineate unsafe areas

For Work with Mortar

Access to water

Disposal of cleanup wastewater

Waterproof storage for cement

Insurance

Homeowner's policy with existing coverage and options to obtain additional coverage for construction

Certificates of insurance from subcontractors

Right: Even adding a small backyard patio requires that you check for buried utilities.

PLANNING YOUR PROJECT

2

Become a Soil Sleuth

The quality of the soil is the most critical existing condition for the long-term stability of your stonework. It's especially important to know its history if you want to build a large project. Tall walls and retainer walls need adequate and properly compacted fill. Without it, the stonework will sag or creep and eventually fall apart.

Test holes are sometimes enough to determine the presence of fill and other characteristics of the soil. Soil that digs easily is likely to be either uncompacted fill or too sandy to safely support large stonework. Undisturbed gravelly soils are ideal. They require the least amount of base, backfill material, and supplemental drainage. Any other soil type is likely to require additional excavation and replacement with more stable material.

Above: For stability, construct walls on firm, well-draining soil.

Left: Placing dry-laid patios and specimen stones requires shallow excavations.

Opposite: For an interesting design variation, combine a stone wall with traditional fencing.

Estimating Time

If you need to estimate how long it will take to install your project, ask a mason how long it would take an experienced person to complete each of the project steps. Depending on your skill level, add anywhere from 100 to 200 percent of the time that the mason estimates. Or use the technique of estimating time as best you can and then doubling that figure.

If your soil drains poorly, you may need to divert water by creating a swale or installing a French drain (also called drainage tile).

Minimize Excavation Surprises. Before you begin to excavate, explore your site. Check for large rocks, ledge, and unusual fill in the areas you want to excavate or reshape. Believe it or not, it's possible to find such things as old sidewalk curbing buried a foot under a suburban lawn.

To check an area, drive an iron bar to the estimated excavation depth every 3 to 4 feet in the entire area. Wherever possible, modify your design to work with existing large rocks and ledge. It's expensive to blast and move massive rocks—especially when uncovering them can instead reveal a landscaping treasure.

Erosion. In stonework, erosion concerns usually aren't about soil loss, but there is concern that a heavy rain will collapse a bank, leaving you with a muddy mess. Preventive measures can minimize or eliminate erosion problems. For small- to moderate-sized projects, dig ditches and place hay-bale dikes to redirect water. Cover exposed soil, including piles of soil for backfilling or grading, with landscape fabric or plastic. To temporarily protect dry soil from wind erosion, lay weed barrier fabric over the exposed soil and anchor it with rocks, soil, concrete blocks, or wood.

Local regulations may require preventive measures, although residential projects are usually exempt from erosion control regulations. When in doubt, check with your municipal building office.

Create Site Drawings

Drawings help you plan, solve problems, test ideas, communicate, and organize your site management activities. Their necessity and usefulness depends on the size of the project, your work style, and your ability. People with extraordinary spatial abilities can build complex constructions—even entire buildings—without a single drawing. The rest of us, though, need drawings to keep the details of the project straight and the project organized.

Simple Plans. For straightforward uncomplicated projects, use field notes and sketches from the site evaluation to create a set of plan and elevation drawings. Your plan drawing includes fixed points such as specimen plants, buildings, and utility lines as well as the project footprint and any anticipated new drainage lines. On the elevation drawing indicate features such as grade changes, depth of buried utilities, and anticipated excavation and fill requirements.

For projects with complicated grade changes, you

Left: Large projects, such as a long wall, require building space, a delivery area, and a material storage area.

Developing a Site Plan

Typical Plat Map

Customized Site Plan

Be a Good Neighbor

Accidents happen so it is a good idea to anticipate how a borrowed access or storage area might be damaged. For example, excavation equipment can tear up lawn; a load of boulders dumped on the road can damage blacktop; and dense materials such as crushed stone, soil, or plants will kill underlying vegetation in as little as a week. Avoid problems by making a written agreement for the use of a neighbor's—or the town's—property. A municipality may have a form and process for such agreements, but you'll need to draft one for a neighbor.

The agreement should include:

◆ Start and completion dates
◆ Description of the area, including pictures from several angles prior to using it
◆ Description of how you plan on using the property
◆ A clause to restore the land to its former condition. Check with your insurance company ahead of time so that you can answer liability insurance questions

may want to use plan and elevation overlays on your "existing conditions" drawings. These can help you anticipate troublesome transitions or space constraints.

How Much Is Enough? A master plan for high-use areas, excavation and grading plans, construction details, and planting plans reduce errors and help you visualize the process and the finished project. The number of drawings you make and the details you include are a matter of personal preference.

Your plans can't be too accurate. Check measurements a few days after you record them or, even better, have someone else check them. Make it a habit to double-check measurements throughout a project. If you have more than one set of drawings, it's important to note changes on all copies. To avoid confusion, date the drawings whenever you make changes.

Below: For small projects, use simple field notes or sketches as a guide for building and estimating materials.

PLANNING YOUR PROJECT

2

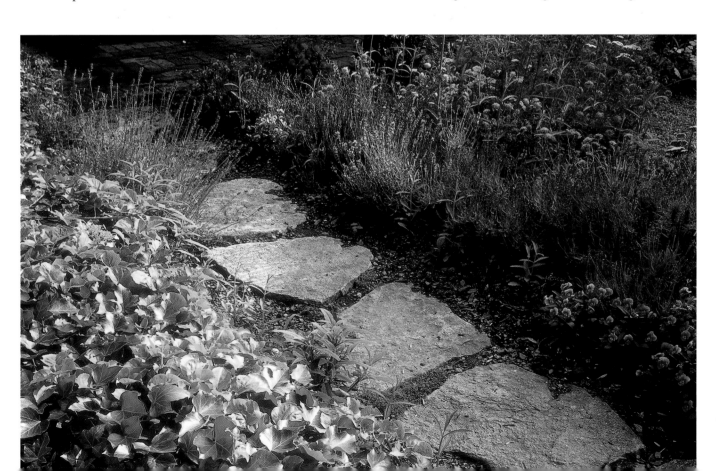

Managing the Work Site

Site management refers to organizing all the details that determine whether or not a project can proceed efficiently and safely. Imagine discovering halfway through a project that you must move several tons of stone because it's preventing access to a part of the work area. Similarly, it's pretty frustrating to realize that you could use a backhoe—instead of a wheelbarrow—to move backfill if you'd only put the piles in a different spot.

To avoid scenarios like this, walk through the steps of your project on the plan drawings and on the site itself. Use a tape measure and flagging ribbon to lay out features and mark critical locations, and talk to the delivery driver, mason, and anyone else who will need access. An equipment operator's criteria for safe, adequate working conditions may not be the same as yours. Steep terrain, water, mud, and unknowns about buried utilities can easily turn into delays.

Use Your Drawing. If your site is complicated, use a copy of your plan drawing to indicate, in scale, storage and delivery areas and where equipment can maneuver. Better yet, use marking paint to designate these areas on the site. If you're working in a confined space, the difference between a pile of stone taking up a 10 × 10-foot area or 20 × 20-foot area could be critical.

Right: When building in small space, make sure there is enough room to store materials.

Opposite: Large, elaborate stone projects require detailed design and construction drawings.

Make Organizing Easy

Make two lists for your project. On one, list the parts or steps of the project; on the other, list the purchases and contracted services. Combine the two lists in the order you need to act on them. Do this, and you will have completed a large part of your work plan. To organize large or complex projects, plot the parts of the project and purchases on a timeline.

Professional Expertise

If you are handling the design and management phases of a large project yourself, have a professional who has experience working with stone assess your plans. Many landscape designers, though they may not have the academic training of a landscape architect, are equally knowledgeable about stonework. The expertise of masons and landscape contractors usually lies in installation rather than design; however, many of them have the project management and design skills needed to review plans for a project. In general, you're looking for the opinion of someone with significant experience in the type of stone project you are planning.

Finding a Pro. Locate professionals through word-of-mouth recommendations, direct contact with individuals whose work you have seen and liked, or you can ask at a garden center or stone supplier for recommendations. Although it may take time, be as diligent in finding someone to advise you as you would be in hiring him or her to do the actual work. Examine his or her portfolio; ask for and check references. Meet with the professionals to discuss your project. You can expect to pay between $35 and $100 an hour for a professional review of your plans.

Final Checks. With your site plan in hand, mentally walk through the steps of the project as you physically walk the site. A walk-through is a good way to catch overlooked parts of a project or forgotten purchases.

Mark critical locations with grade stakes and flagging ribbon, spray paint, or weather-resistant markers; it can be difficult to find these locations once you alter the terrain. If a project will take several months or longer, keep a keyed map with measurements taken from fixed points. Take photos to create a record for future renovations and as documentation if you sell the property.

The Budget as a Planning Aid

Even though you might not think of it this way, a budget is a useful planning aid. Because you develop it as you create the plan, the budget often contains the most comprehensive list of materials and services that you'll need for the project. One planning strategy is to work from a detailed budget to create your work plan. Conversely, a good budget can serve as a cross-reference to anything you might have overlooked while planning your project. No matter how you use the project budget beyond its cost-accounting function, you'll find that the more detailed you make it, the more useful it is.

Opposite: You won't need detailed drawings for this type of wall, but you must make plans to store the stones.

Right: Large stones such as these must be delivered to the site by heavy equipment.

Below: Drawing up a detailed budget can help you plan most projects, no matter how simple.

Typical Budget Categories

Budgets have a way of clarifying goals like nothing else can. Use these general categories to help finalize your project budget. Few projects include all of the categories listed here; choose the ones that apply to your project.

Budget Categories

- Permits
- Removal of existing plants to hold for replanting or disposal
- Removal of excess sod and soil
- Care of plants during construction
- Stone by cubic yards or square feet
- Specimen stones
- Base and/or backfill crushed rock or sand in cubic yards
- Other project materials
- Equipment rental
- Tool purchases
- Sales taxes
- Drainage changes
- Erosion control
- Trucking or other costs to get stone on site
- Temporary protection of work area
- Temporary roadway or access
- New or relocated water, electrical, or telecom lines
- Cleanup costs
- Disposal of excess stone
- Site remediation
- Design fees
- Contractor and subcontractor fees for earth-moving, moving stone, and related landscaping
- Consultation, contracted design, or installation services
- Insurance
- Change in property tax (Ask an assessor how landscaping improvements are valued.)
- Contingencies—a minimum 20 percent of the total project budget

(If you purchase materials six months or more after drawing up the budget, increase estimated costs or the contingency category 5 to 10 percent.)

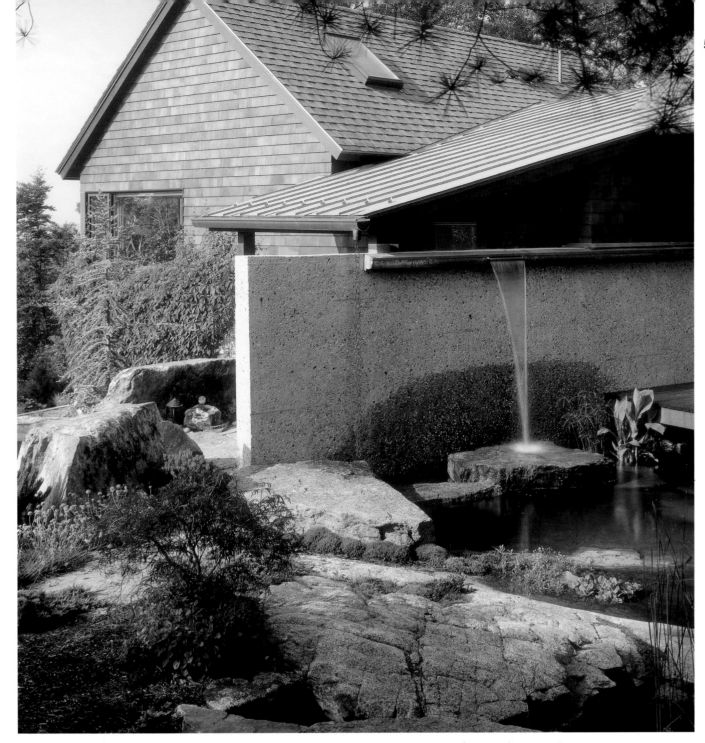

Opposite left: Large specimen stones support brightly colored flowers on a hillside.

Opposite right: A path of flagstone slabs winds through a mature garden.

Above: Large stones found on site become part of the overall landscape design.

How Much Will It Cost?

When you put cost figures to a project, it culminates the planning phase and sets the installation process in motion. If you are your own general contractor, many businesses will give you a contractor's price and an account for the duration of your project. Prices for construction materials fluctuate, and some suppliers will guarantee you a price if you make the purchase within a given period of time. Insist on written estimates or bids from designers, contractors, and subcontractors for any work they perform. Agree on the terms for payment beforehand. Use the budget categories in "Typical Budget Categories," opposite page, to help you finalize your project budget.

CHAPTER 3

Stone

As a Building Material

The stone for your project can come from one of a number of sources, including quarries and garden centers. But don't overlook other sources, such as your own backyard, the fields near your home, streams, and demolition or blasting sites. In many of those areas, the stone is free. Due to obvious shipping and storage problems, most stone is quarried and sold locally, although special orders are possible. The yellow pages of your telephone book will list local stone suppliers.

Stone Classifications

Masons and builders describe stone in different ways, depending on the context. You'll find it classified by its geological type, trade names, or the dimensions or shapes commonly used in construction and landscaping. For example, granite is a trade name for a specific type of igneous rock—the geologic classification. For landscaping, granite is sold as pavers, blocks or ashlar, steps, specimen stones, rubble, and crushed rock in a variety of sizes. Go to a quarry or stone yard, and you will see examples of stone that are cut in uniform shapes with smooth surfaces, called dressed stone, and the same stone in a more natural, unfinished state, called rough. (See "Terms for Stone," opposite.)

Below: A fieldstone wall complements the more formal structures behind it.

Terms for Stone

The following are common words used in the landscaping trade to describe different types of stone. You may also find other words used that are specific to a geographic region. Visit a stoneyard to learn about the types of stone available to you.

Ashlar   Any stone cut to a square or rectangular shape in either random or uniform sizes. Also, a pattern for laying courses of rectangular blocks of stone.

Belgian blocks   Stone cut in square or rectangular shapes, usually about the size of a large brick, and used for paving.

Chinkers   Small, irregular-sized stones used to fill in gaps in a wall.

Cobblestone   Small rounded stone used for paving. Also, any small-dimension milled stone that is used for paving.

Cut stone   Any stone that has been milled or worked by hand to a specific shape or dimension.

Crushed rock   Small-dimension material available in a range of colors and sizes with either a smooth or angular surface.

Dressed stone   Usually quarried stone that has been squared off on all sides and has a smooth face.

Face   The exposed side of a stone.

Fieldstone   Stone as it is found in the natural environment.

Flagging   Paving for walks or patios made from flagstone.

Flagstone   Any stone milled to a uniform thickness of 1–2 inches to use for walk and patio surfaces. Flagstone is available in uniform rectangular shapes or in random shaped pieces that are fitted together like a jigsaw puzzle.

Pavers   Any stone milled to a uniform size and shape, typically about the size of a brick, and used to surface walkways and patios.

Quarry dressed   A term for stone that is squared off on all sides but has a rough face. Sometimes called semidressed stone.

River stones   Small- to medium-sized collected stones that are worn or rounded from water.

Rough stone   Stone as it comes from the quarry.

Rubble   Stone blasted on a construction site or pieces left over from cutting quarried stone. Also, any low-grade stone used for fill in a stone wall.

Semidressed   A term for stone that is squared off on two or more sides but has a rough face.

Specimen stone   A stone with unusual color, surface, or form that is used alone or in an arrangement of other speciman stones for its sculptural or decorative qualities.

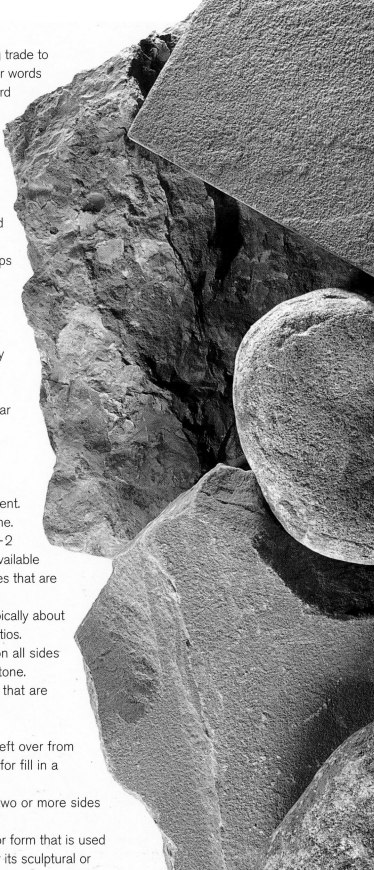

Stone Names. The composition of geological stone types varies widely from one place to another, as do the trade names given to each type of stone. The geological classification is sometimes used as a trade name, or a quarry may make up a trade name. Wilmington Schist refers to a specific type of metamorphic rock quarried in southern Vermont. It also happens to be a trade name.

Moss rock is a common name for a type of stone found in southern and central New Mexico. Although the name does not really convey any information about the stone, New Mexico masons know it as a locally quarried type of sandstone. However, someone could make pavers out of moss rock, and market them under the trade name "South Sun Pavers." Sometimes a photograph or a visual inspection is the only way to accurately identify the stone type.

Evaluating Stone

When selecting stone for a project, you need to determine whether the type of stone would be appropriate for the planned use and whether the stone type itself is fairly uniform or extremely variable.

Determining whether a stone is appropriate is a straightforward matter of looking at its aesthetic and structural characteristics. Aesthetic characteristics such as color, texture, size, and shape contribute to the overall look of your project. If color uniformity is important, select a type of stone that can be reliably tooled or shaped without revealing other colors. Structural characteristics are critical for ease of construction and the durability of the installation. You may need to consider porosity, mechanical strength, quality of building surfaces, and how easy it is to cut, split, or shape the stone.

Left: The variations in color, size, and shape contribute to this fountain's unique design.

Above: Choose stone for your project based on its color, texture, size, and workability.

Above: Visit projects you admire to learn how to put the natural variations of stone to good use in your project.

Below: When ordering stone, It is best to bring photos and samples of the stone you want to the stone yard.

Variations in Stone. Stone is never homogeneous; there can be variations in quality even among different stones from the same quarry. It takes vigilance, visual inspection, and an occasional whack of a hammer to evaluate the quality of a specific type of stone. If you can personally select the stone for your project, do it.

Some stone can appear to be good building stone but begin to crumble within a few years. Be cautious if stone seems under priced. And ask the supplier for the names of masons who use it. Take the time to call and ask the masons about their experience with the stone.

If you are unsure about the suitability of a local stone, you can sometimes find information about it through the Extension Service or a U.S. Soil Conservation office. Masons, designers, and landscape architects who use natural stone are often familiar with the qualities of stone common to an area.

Small-Dimension Materials

Small-dimension materials such as gravel, crushed rock, pea stone, and bedding sand are sometimes unavailable from building stone suppliers. Visit sand and gravel yards to become familiar with the colors, sizes, and surface qualities of those that are available. Take pictures or bring along sturdy sacks or crates to take samples home.

Gravel is an excellent base for many stone projects because it provides stability and creates good drainage. Ask your supplier about the availability of gravel that packs and drains well. Each quarry uses different names for its gravel and stone products. Keep a written record for comparison shopping and ordering.

Price, Availability, and Quantity

All other things being equal, the more dressed stone is, the higher the price. For paving, large, uniformly shaped pieces are typically more expensive than smaller or randomly shaped pieces of the same type and quality.

Because so much stone sold for landscaping is available in more than one form, ask a supplier or quarry if it is available as a special order if you don't find what you want. Almost all commercially available stone is sold by the cubic yard, either loose or by the pallet. Specimen stones may be priced individually without regard to measurements.

How Much Do You Need? To figure out how much stone you need, first calculate the cubic volume of stone for the project. Then add a percentage for waste. The amount of extra stone you need to order depends on the type of stone and the application. You don't have waste with specimen stones of

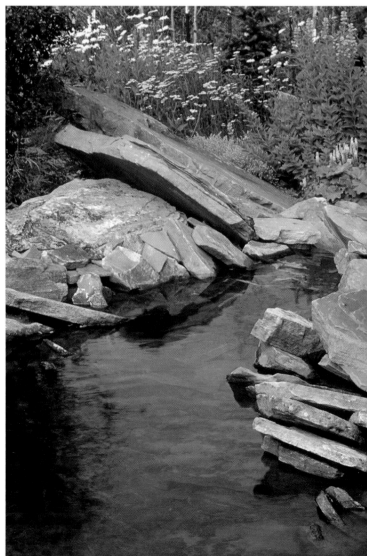

The Cost of Stone

Factors that affect the price of stone include

- Type of stone
- Building qualities
- Point of origin
- Delivery charges

Using Leftover Stone

If you are building a stone wall, use waste stone to fill the space between two wythes, or it can be used as fill behind a retainer wall. Smaller dimension leftover stone can also be put to good use for narrow maintenance paths through garden areas.

Try to get a second opinion when you are deciding how much stone to order. An informed opinion can minimize both shortages and overages, as well as save you problems with disposing of extra material. The supplier or a mason familiar with the stone and the application can help you calculate accurately.

course, and you can minimize waste for sand and gravel with good calculations. Brick and other small uniform materials have as little as 5 percent waste. If you build with natural fieldstone, you may order up to 50 percent extra. How much you'll need depends on the quality of the stone, what you are building, the look you want, and how much time you are willing to spend on shaping stones to fit.

Opposite far left: The rounded edges of river stones make them good choices for water features.

Left: Large specimen stones provide a rugged-looking setting for this backyard water feature.

Above: Collect samples of small stones so that you can experiment with combining colors and textures.

Below: A Japanese-inspired raked gravel garden can offer a spot for quiet contemplation.

Guidelines for Delivery

Think about where to place the materials before they arrive. You'll need to get to them easily, but you want to avoid obstructing access to the rest of the site. If you can efficiently store and access all the materials for your project simultaneously, ask whether delivery costs will be less if you take delivery of all of them at the same time.

To guarantee that the materials will be placed where you want them, be there when the delivery truck arrives. If the delivery truck dumps your loose stone, some stones will break. Many more will get marred and, depending on where they're dumped, dirty. If this is unacceptable, unload the stone by hand or with a bucket loader. Use a power washer to dull scuff marks and clean off dirt and stone dust.

Below: For large projects, ask the delivery driver to space the pallets along the length of the project.

Below right: Some stone yards will set large stones like these as part of the delivery process.

Found Stone

If you don't have a supply of stone on your property, you can collect or salvage stone as an alternative to buying it from a retail yard or quarry. "Rocks" that you once barely noticed or may have considered a nuisance suddenly become valuable. Be sure to obtain the owner's written permission when removing stone from someone's property.

Stone Sources

- Old stone walls and foundations
- Abandoned quarries and mill sites
- Scrap piles at operating quarries
- Areas that have been logged
- Building contractors and earthmoving equipment operators
- Town and state road crews
- Developers and development sites*
- Demolition sites and wrecking companies*
- Blasting sites and contractors*
- Abandoned buildings
- Ads in local papers

*Expect time constraints when you are removing stone from development and demolition sites.

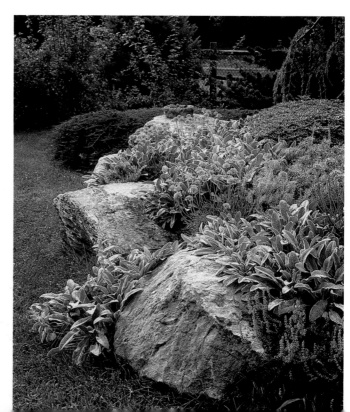

Delivery Services. When you order large stones, ask whether the trucker will set them in place. Although companies charge an additional fee for this service based on the amount of time it will take, it's almost always worth it. One way or another, setting stones that weigh 300-plus pounds requires equipment or much muscle and time. Remember that a stone that measures a mere 2 cubic feet can weigh this much; larger stones are much heavier. If you opt to set stones as part of the delivery, prepare the site and, if possible, decide ahead of time how to orient the stones.

3

STONE AS A BUILDING MATERIAL

Above: Search out old stone walls and abandoned structures as sources of free or inexpensive stone.

Left: In many parts of the country, the area around your home will yield a treasure trove of stone.

Below: Combine plants with stone to create areas that will change with the seasons.

Learn from the Stone

Get to know your stone. Practice on the same type stone you will use in your project. Experiment with how it responds when you split, cut, or chisel it. The better you understand it, the better you'll be able to work it.

For many projects, the quality and overall look of your work depends on the placement of each and every stone. This can be a challenge with any project, but it is particularly difficult when you are building something like a wall. Not only do you have to consider the aesthetic factors, you also have to think about its structural integrity.

Some masons seem to have a natural affinity for placement. But with patience and practice, anyone can cultivate an eye for correctly placing stone. If you take your time with this part of the work, your stonework will turn out to be the pleasing project you originally envisioned. Don't expect to get it right the first time. As with any craft, good stonework takes patience and practice.

Below right: Don't try this at home. Stone sculptures are fascinating, but structures such as this usually require the expertise of a professional.

Opposite: Before starting any project, especially a complicated one such as this, experiment with the stone you will be using.

Formulas You'll Need

Square feet: length x width in feet.

Cubic feet: length x width x depth. Use decimals for fractions of a foot: 0.25 for 3 inches, 0.33 for 4 inches, 0.5 for 6 inches. For example, a 4-inch sand bed for a 14 x 20-foot patio would be 14 x 20 x 0.33 = 92.4 cubic feet.

Cubic yards: divide the number of cubic feet by 27. So 92.4 divided by 27 = 3.42 yards, or about 3½ yards.

To calculate the volume of a pile of material, such as a pile of excess soil that you may need to remove from your property, think of the pile as a tapered cone. To calculate volume of the cone: V = pi (3.14) x radius squared (radius is ½ the diameter) x height, divided by 3.

For example, if the pile is 4 feet high and the diameter at the base is 8 feet, multiply 3.14 x 16 (radius squared is 4 x 4) = 50.24 x 4 (height) = 201, divided by 3 = 67 cubic feet. To get cubic yards, divide cubic feet by 27. Using the example above, 67 divided by 27 = 2.48, or about 2½ cubic yards.

Smart Tip

A Real-Life Stone Lesson

A mason I know set a 3 ton (about 3 x 4 x 3 feet) specimen stone at his home. He knew the stone straddled the sewer pipe, but he calculated that the surrounding ground would take the brunt of the load. And for several years it did. But on the morning that he and his family were to depart for a vacation, the sewer pipe collapsed and flooded the basement. After making the repairs, he relocated the stone. He tells the story as a lesson and reminder of the tremendous, constant weight of stone.

CHAPTER 4

Tools &
Techniques

Working with stone is similar to assembling a three-dimensional jigsaw puzzle. Fortunately, the stone you select and the tools you use to work the stone can help make the task easier. By training your eye to evaluate each stone—its size, building surfaces, and structural qualities—you can decide where the stone fits in your project. By choosing the right tool because of ease of handling and cutting ability, you will not only complete your project but enjoy the rewards of working with stone.

Tools

The specific tools you will use depend on both the project itself and the type of stone you are using. Besides general construction and landscaping tools, you'll use tools to shape, split, and cut stone. Other tools will help you move and set large stones. For mortared projects, you will also need tools for mixing and applying mortar.

Cutting and shaping tools, such as mason's hammers, chisels and points, circular saw blades, and right-angle grinder blades take the most abuse. Both disposable masonry blades and diamond blades are commonly available for circular saws. The type of blade you choose depends in part on the amount of cutting you have to do. If the work involves a lot of shaping and splitting, you'll need a couple of chisels and points. Sharpen them regularly on a grinding stone, or invest in a 1½-inch carbide chisel that does not require sharpening.

Above: Quarried stone set directly into the lawn forms a curving path across the garden.

Below: Many stonework projects, such as the dry-laid wall shown here, require few specialized tools.

Tool Practice

Smart Tip

If you are unfamiliar with any of the tools you'll be using, practice with them before beginning the project.

Tools for Stonework

Construction Tools

Measuring tape

Marking device, pencil, nail

4-ft. level, string level

Circular saw

Right-angle grinder

Framing or claw hammer

10-lb. sledgehammer

Grade stakes

Mason's line

Hammer holster

Tool belt or vest

Circular Saw & Masonry Blade

Tools to Work Stone

Mason's hammer – to shape or split stone

Brick hammer – to shape or split stone (similar to a mason's hammer, not as versatile)

Chisels – to split stone and cut flagging

Points – to chip and direct the force of impact

Mash hammer – to hit chisels and points

Rubber mallet – to set flagging and stepping-stones

Toothed chisel – to refine the shape of softer stones such as limestone or sandstone

Bush hammer – to smooth or dress irregular surfaces in soft stone

Masonry blades – for circular saw and right-angle grinder

Wet kits – for worm-driven circular saws

Mason's Hammer

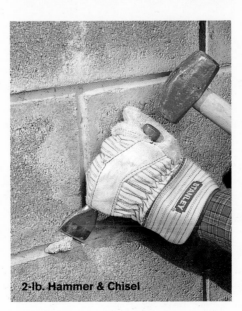
2-lb. Hammer & Chisel

Landscaping Tools

Shovels

Digging spade

Rakes

Wheelbarrow

Tamper

Equipment to Rent

Power tamper

Masonry saw

Bobcat or tractor/bucket

Power washer

Stone-Moving Tools

Come-along

Platforms and pipe rollers

Tripod

Safety Equipment

Goggles

Gloves

Upper forearm support air cast

Steel-toed shoes

Ear plugs

Dust mask

Kneepads

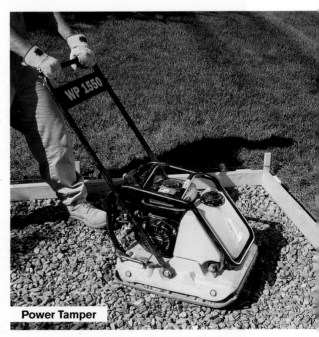
Power Tamper

Leveling Tools

If you can borrow a transit, do it, especially if your project requires extensive grading.

Line levels are inexpensive, but they provide inaccurate readings if not used correctly. The longer the distance you are leveling, the less accurate they are. If you use one:

• Use mason's line for your string
• Pull the line as taut as possible
• Place the level in the exact center of the span
• Reverse the level and split any difference between the two measurements for the most accurate reading

To check the accuracy of any level, use it to take a reading; reverse the level, and take the reading again. If both readings are the same, the level is accurate.

Tool Preferences

People develop personal preferences for stone-shaping tools based on comfort and control. For example, you might find a chisel and hammer more comfortable to use than an all-purpose 2-pound mason's hammer. Some hammers have impact-absorbing handles, which make them more comfortable to use. A dead-blow hammer delivers more impact than a conventional sledge of the same size. Homeowner-grade circular saws and right-angle grinders equipped with diamond blades can save time, but these tools won't last if you cut a lot of stone or make long cuts. If you have a lot of cutting and shaping to do, you can use a chisel and hammer or rent industrial cutting tools. Specific techniques and tools to shape, split, and cut stone are discussed in the projects beginning in the next chapter.

Preventive Tool Maintenance. Over time, the heads of chisels and points can start to mushroom from repeated hits with a hammer. Grind the edges of the head to reduce the risk of cuts from sharp

Opposite: Specimen stones placed in this type of arrangement usually do not require any cutting or shaping.

Above: Even if you purchase dressed stone, you may still need to do some cutting to complete your project.

Below right: When sorting stones after delivery, arrange them into groups of similar characteristics, such as size or shape.

edges. If a sledge or mason's hammer has a wooden handle, wrap wire around it a few inches near the head, and wrap the wire with a strip of tire inner-tube as if it were a bandage. It's easy to lose hammers, chisels, and points in a stone pile, so paint these tools bright orange.

Working with Stone

With the exception of placing specimen stones, the following steps apply to working with stone. While the steps may be the same no matter which type of stone you use, the work is most challenging when the stones are irregularly shaped. Without experience, it may be hard to believe that the quality and overall look of your work really comes down to the structural and aesthetic decisions you make to place each and every stone. This is the challenge of stonework.

Some professional masons seem to have a natural affinity for placing stone. It takes patience and practice, but it is certainly possible for the novice to develop an eye for stonework.

Before you Begin

The stone is your teacher, so it is in your best interest to become familiar with its character. Experiment with how the stone responds when you split, cut, or chisel it. Consider how variations in its color or texture can enhance your project.

Sorting. After your stone is delivered, sort it for specific uses. If you are building a freestanding wall with fieldstone, sort for large bottom course stones, corner stones, bond stones, cap stones, shim stones, and rubble to fill between wythes. Sort the remaining stones into two or three groups by size.

Every stone has a place. As you sort stone, you build a memory of the stones that you will use later. All through the sorting process, you should be looking for stones with specific structural traits, such as uniform thickness or right-angle faces. You will find yourself selecting others for aesthetic properties that can establish the look or rhythm of your project.

4

TOOLS AND TECHNIQUES

Choosing Stone During Construction. During construction, evaluate each stone again, but this time to determine the best surfaces for a base, top, face, and sides. Assess the degree of flatness and right angles to the face. Then evaluate how this stone fits to the ones adjacent to it.

For example, in wall construction, you have to consider four building surfaces: the two lateral faces and the top and bottom ones. Besides the stone's surfaces, you'll also need to consider how the load is distributed as well as whether the fit of the stone helps to create a flat bed for the next course. (See "Understanding Gravity," right.)

Another way to select a stone is to evaluate the shape of the space and look for that shape in the stone pile. With practice, you can intentionally create spaces that use the stones you have. (See "Stone Selection," opposite.)

Pay as much attention to the origin of your stones as to the technical considerations when you are placing them. For example, if you have a stone that was partially buried, it will have a distinct color change at the soil line. If you turned this stone 90 degrees, you'd diminish its natural look and aesthetic appeal, even if the shape works beautifully

Establishing a Rhythm. Designers use the term rhythm to refer to the way stones of varying sizes and types create a pattern that, though not necessarily geometric, is intentional. Often subtle, rhythm is crucial to the unity and aesthetic appeal of your project. Use rhythm as one criterion to select stones: place them purposefully. Even a skilled mason who is experimenting with a particular effect sometimes dismantles and rebuilds a section of stonework looking for a sustaining rhythm.

Supporting Stones

Construction Tip

You must support stones while you are shaping them. You can hold small stones against your leg or in your lap. When you are working on a larger stone or one that needs a lot of shaping, a sand pile or bag of sand is handy. The sand conforms to the stone's shape and supports the stone at whatever angle you place it.

Understanding Gravity

If your stonework is to last, you must understand the force of gravity and how it will affect your project. If you don't consider the effects of gravity, vertical constructions can shift and start to fall apart within a few years.

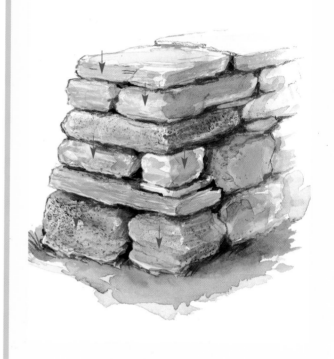

Shaping Skills

Deciding whether to hunt for a stone that is a good fit or shape one that nearly fits is often more a matter of work style and aesthetics than of necessity or expediency. For example, in walls and patios, how much the stone is shaped will determine, at least in part, joint size and naturalness—both significant aesthetic elements.

Before you begin to shape a stone, evaluate it again—this time for hardness, grain, presence of fractures, and composition. All of these factors can affect a stone's structural integrity and how a stone will break. Shaping stone is similar to splitting firewood or using a hand plane. Grain and imperfections dictate angle, force, and the quantity you remove.

Work with the Stone. Work with the grain and fractures, chipping off a little at a time. To locate fine fractures, wet the stone and allow it to dry. A fracture will remain wet longer than the rest of the stone. As you become familiar with how a type of stone reacts to the impact of hammer and chisel, you can adjust both the amount removed and the power of your swing. Listen for auditory clues as you work, too. Sometimes you can salvage a stone if you notice soon enough that it is not breaking where you want it to break.

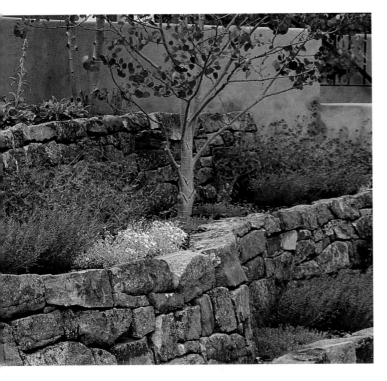

Above: It takes practice, but as you become comfortable working with stone, you will begin to select stones for different parts of your project with confidence.

Stone Orientation

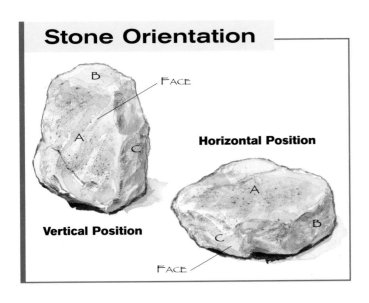

Stone Selection

4 Options for Completing a Wall Section

Order of Work

Begin your project in the least visible place. By the time you get to the portion that is most noticeable, your technique will have improved.

Dressed Stone

Many quarries will dress stone so that you don't need to do much trimming to build with it. This stone costs more and creates a less natural look than found, blasted, or rough quarried stone. But the time it takes to fit the stone and complete your project is considerably shortened.

Cutting Tools. You can cut dressed and semi-dressed flagging, step, and wall stone with a chisel and hammer, circular saws, or pneumatic cutting tools. Or you can split them as they've been split for thousands of years—with feather wedges. Each method changes the appearance of the stone's face, giving you good reason to choose one method over another.

Sometimes you need to break up large stones to make rubble fill or shims, especially in freestanding wall construction. To break up a large stone without regard for the shapes of the pieces, hit it hard with the largest sledgehammer you can comfortably swing, and wear safety goggles while you do it.

Experience Counts. Learning how to see the potential and limitations of a stone is challenging. Strong visualizing abilities can help you gain a working knowledge of stone more easily. But with time and practice, anyone, at any skill level, can cultivate an eye for choosing and placing a suitable stone. Patience, studied observation, and an appreciation for the effort that goes into good stonework make the work more enjoyable.

Far left: Using wedges and shims, called feathers, is a traditional method of splitting large stones.

Left: Modern stone cutters often use pneumatic tools to cut and shape large stones.

Above: Here is a unique use of small-dimension stones and edging materials.

Opposite: Plan your project to keep cutting to a minimum, as was the case for this patio and walkway.

Safety Tips for Working with Stone

- Wear steel-toed shoes, especially if you're working with large pieces of stone.
- Wear a disposable face mask and goggles to cut stone.
- Wear eye protection when chiseling stone or using power tools.
- Rope off large holes or steep grade changes, and mark them with flagging ribbon or brightly colored strips of cloth.
- Wear rubber boots, protective clothing, gloves, and goggles if you work with concrete. Pro-
longed contact with fresh concrete will irritate your skin.
- Use a tool pouch to carry hand tools, especially chisels.
- Keep your chisels sharp.
- Know the limits of your tools. Don't force them to do what they were not intended to do.
- Practice using tools with which you are unfamiliar before beginning your project.
- Know your physical limits. Use pry bars, skids, winches, and the like to move large stones.

Above: Mortared walls, walks, and patios tend to be more formal than dry-laid stonework.

Below: Mortared projects such as this one require a drainage system.

Mortared Stonework

Although mortared stonework can cost up to twice as much as the same work dry laid, safety or aesthetic reasons make it preferable in some applications. Avoid using mortar as a substitute for fitting stone to stone or as an attempt to defy gravity.

For home improvement and landscaping, mortared stonework is more popular in dry, mild climates where the installation costs are lower. But considerations other than cost are also important. Even in climates without frost, the natural movement of the earth can, over time, cause mortar to crack. Mortar exposed to weather deteriorates before the stone. Eventually it will need to be renewed for aesthetic reasons or, in some cases, to keep the stonework intact. Mortared stonework requires supplemental drainage, too. Water can't move through mortared stonework as it does through dry-laid stone.

How to Mix Mortar

Use a wheelbarrow, mason's mixing box, or piece of plywood to mix your mortar. Combine one part portland cement with three parts mortar sand. Thoroughly mix the dry ingredients using a hoe. Form them into a mound with a well in the middle. Pour clean water into the well, and gradually mix the dry ingredients with the water, working from the center of the mound to the edges. The amount of water will vary with the weather conditions and the amount of moisture in the sand. Measure the amount you use to get a sense of how much you need for each batch.

The mortar should be stiff enough to support the stones but wet enough to spread easily. The following can help you get the right consistency:

- If water seeps out of the mortar around the edges, it is too wet.

- Test-set a stone on a piece of plywood. If the mortar cannot support the stone with at least a 1-inch bed of mortar, it is too wet.

- Palm a lump of mortar in your hand. If it holds together and has a smooth uniform shape, it's wet enough.

Mortaring Tricks and Techniques

- Mortar is irritating to the skin. Wear gloves, and wash off mortar immediately if it gets on your skin.
- Mortar dries quickly. Work with small batches, no more than the amount you can use within an hour or so. Shade the mortar from direct sun, especially during midday, and cover it with plastic if the weather is hot or windy.
- Begin by working with an area large enough for two to four stones. Increase the size of the work area as your skill improves.
- Use tarps or cardboard to keep the foundation clean. Use plywood to distribute the load if you need to stand on freshly laid stones.
- Slow curing is important. Keep finished work damp by misting it and covering it with plastic for up to seven days.
- Clean the surface of stones that get spattered with mortar before the mortar hardens. Use a sponge and clean water.
- Mortar stains some types of stone. Check with a supplier, or test your stone for susceptibility to staining.

Above: A mortared patio installation allows for the creation of precise patterns over large areas.

Extra Stone

If you are building with an unusual type of stone, stockpile a small quantity of various sizes. It is nice to know that you have replacement stones if an accident ever occurs.

Living with Stone

Although stonework installations require little or no maintenance to remain strong and sturdy, some attention will be required to enhance your use and enjoyment.

For safety, hose or sweep walking surfaces to remove vegetative litter and dirt, especially on steeply sloping paths.

Soil pockets in stonework are ideal for planting small ground covers or ornamentals. Unfortunately, blown-in weed seeds can also grow in them. If you can't plant the pockets right away, cover them with plastic and mulch until you are ready to plant. Once the plants mature, it's more difficult for weed seeds to establish themselves.

Mosses tend to thrive in environments with high humidity, moderate to high moisture levels, and some shade. However, some species will tolerate other types of environments. If you want moss to grow on your stonework, search for mosses that are growing in conditions similar to those of your stonework.

Moss Milkshake. To transplant moss, try this gardener's trick. Crumble a tuft of moss with soil attached in a blender. Add equal parts water and buttermilk, and process until the mixture is the con-

Eliminate Moss

Moss isn't always desirable. If you want to discourage moss on your stonework, apply a diluted solution of hydrogen peroxide (½ cup of 3% hydrogen peroxide to 1 gallon of water) to all the stone surfaces until they are wet. Reapply the solution as needed to keep the surface wet for two minutes. If necessary, rinse to remove any residue.

sistency of cream soup (add more water if necessary). Spread the mixture where you want moss to grow. Keep the area moist until the moss is established.

Stone Displacement

Even with your best efforts, some of your stones may get displaced. Normal settling or even an accident can cause this.

Dry-laid stonework is more easily rebuilt than mortared projects. Repeated displacement that is not caused by an accident is a sign of an inadequate foundation, too little backfill, or poor drainage.

Protect your Plants

Plants almost always suffer if they are close to the area where you are installing a stonework project. Not only does most stonework require some excavation, it also adds tremendous concentrated weight to the underlying soil. Nearby roots are likely to be damaged while you're working.

Ninety percent of a plant's feeder roots are in the top foot of soil—the area most often disturbed by stonework. Although some controversy exists about where a plant's primary feeder roots are located in relation to the trunk, horticulturists agree that compacting or severing a plant's roots can temporarily reduce vitality or trigger a gradual decline.

Left: Consider using plants as borders for your stonework, or grow plants in soil pockets in walls.

Below: Allowing moss to grow between pavers is an attractive and inexpensive way to finish the project.

Temporary Relocations

Create a temporary holding bed for any plants that are in the way or might get damaged during installation. You can safely move many plants, even several species of mature trees. But before you start digging, do some research. Several variables affect a plant's ability to survive transplanting and temporary relocation, including soil type, plant species, time of year, general health, lead time, access, and your capacity to provide care both in a temporary holding area and after the plant is permanently replanted. In the case of large plants, the cost to move them is a significant factor, too. Under the right conditions you can move an 80-foot-tall tree, but it will cost thousands of dollars.

If you need help evaluating whether a plant will survive, consult with a landscaper, arborist, or grower who is knowledgeable about the species you want to move and has experience moving mature plants.

Coddle Displaced Plants. Many species of plants can survive in temporary locations for several years if they have good care. Regardless of your relocation method, keep the plants out of the wind and give them similar or less exposure to sunlight than they had in their former location. They will need more water than normal, especially if they are out of the ground or only partially replanted. Some species, such as those with high moisture requirements or coarse root systems, may benefit from being cut back to minimize transplant shock. Check with a knowledgeable landscaper, arborist, or grower to learn whether this is a good preventive measure for your plants.

Create a Good Home

Dig the plants in the late afternoon or on a cloudy day to reduce the stress they'll experience. After digging, to give them a temporary home, you can

- Set them on the ground in a shady spot. Wrap the rootballs in burlap. Cover rootballs with a thick layer of mulch to shield them from sun and wind, and to retain moisture. Use bark mulch, wood shavings, hay, horse manure mixed with bedding, or evergreen boughs for mulch. Water daily or as needed.
- Partially or completely replant your plants in another location. If you partially replant them, cover the exposed portion of the rootball with mulch.
- Pot the plants. You might have difficulty finding a pot large enough for a tree, but many shrubs can fit into a half-barrel or other large container.

Below left: When planning, remember that stonework can crush tree and shrub roots that are near the surface.

Below: A stone wall serves as a backdrop for statuary and climbing plants.

Above: Consult with a landscape designer or arborist about the effects your project will have on trees and other plants.

Emergency Pruning

If you break any branches, immediately prune them back to a joint or flush with the branch collar.

Saving Sod

To save sod for future replanting, use a square-edged digging spade to cut it into manageable pieces. Although you can roll up larger pieces if soil adheres to the roots, 18-inch squares are manageable for most people. Undercut the sod with 1½ inches of soil. To save the sod, place it on bare ground that has been at least lightly cultivated, fertilize it lightly, and water thoroughly. Continue to provide supplemental watering if rainfall is less than 1 inch a week.

Working Around Mature Trees and Shrubs

Large earthmoving equipment compacts the soil and breaks roots. This alone can kill some plants. To distribute the load from heavy equipment, lay down planks where the equipment will be used. Depending on the disruption to plants on the site, provide preventive or remediation care. Water the plants, divert excess water from the area, and fertilize as needed. Wrap furniture-moving pads around tree trunks to protect the bark from impact.

Above: Changes in drainage patterns may affect plants. Check for signs of stress.

Left: Large projects such as this may require you to move shrubs and trees to another location.

Be a Good Neighbor

Remain aware of the mature plants on properties adjacent to yours. You'll want to provide the same precautions and care to your neighbor's plants as you do to your own. If necessary, let your neighbors know what you are doing and how they can protect their plants.

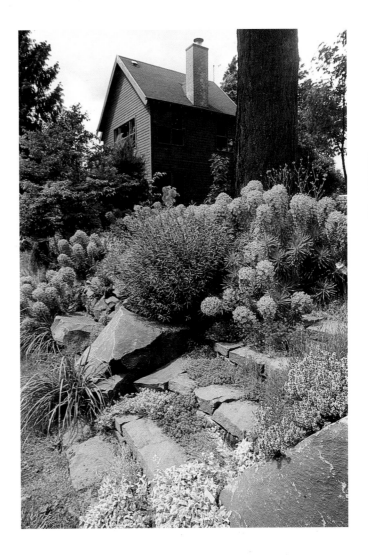

If your excavation comes within 10 feet of a large plant's drip line, you will sever some roots. To reduce shock and minimize stress, cover the ends of exposed roots with mulch, apply a root stimulant either prior to or after excavation, and provide supplemental water. You may be able to purchase a small amount of root stimulant from a nursery stock grower. Watering plants with a diluted seaweed solution can also help them recover from severed roots.

Changing the Grade

Adding or removing soil around a plant can affect the plant's vigor. How much change in grade a plant can tolerate depends on the plant's general health and its adaptability. For example, soft maples (*Acer rubrum*) tolerate dramatic increases in grade, but sugar maples (*Acer saccharum*) do not. Consult a professional to learn how to improve the chances that a mature plant will survive any changes you make.

Altering Natural Watercourses

When you divert water away from stonework or install drainage, you're changing the patterns of natural watercourses. Plants in the area have adapted to these watercourses and may suffer from the changes you've made. Monitor plants that are downhill from areas where you have diverted groundwater or rainfall runoff. Provide supplemental water if plants show signs of stress. Signs of stress include slowed growth rate, change in foliage texture or color, earlier onset of dormancy, and increased pest infestation.

Above right: Adding stonework to a hillside may require replacing some of the original plants.

Right: A dry stream bed and bridge add a decorative touch to this landscape.

CHAPTER 5

Paths &
Walkways

Although paths and walkways direct foot traffic and provide access into and through the landscape, they can fulfill several other landscaping functions. Walkways can divide up large areas, providing more vantage points for viewing gardens. Within a garden, a well-designed path can draw you toward a particular destination. When you use the same material for paths in different parts of the landscape, the paths provide design unity. Paths and walkways also tie preexisting areas to new design elements.

Path and Walkway Design

Paths and walkways can define or create space. For example, a walkway that goes from the driveway to the house can create a planting area between the walk and the side of the house.

The surface quality and overall dimensions of a path or walkway affect its usefulness, so it's important to think about the primary use of the walk early on in the project. Is it to move quickly and directly from one place to another, or to meander slowly as you would through a garden? Do you need a walkway that can accommodate a stroller, walker, or wheel–chair? Do you want to be able to maneuver a garden cart or wheelbarrow along the path? Is it a walk or path you are apt to use barefoot? Asking yourself questions like these will help you figure out what kinds of stone are suitable for your project.

Complement Garden Features

Walkways can complement features such as fences, gates, patios, plantings, and steps. If you consider all the site features together, it will help you make decisions about the location of a walk or path, its design, and the choice of materials to build it. As a general rule of thumb, design paths or walkways to complement the other landscape features in both scale and formality.

Maintenance. Design the walk to make it a pleasure to use with a minimal amount of maintenance. Slope the path to avoid flooding or ponding water. If the path is adjacent to a sloped planting bed, install edging that will keep soil from washing out onto the path stones.

Walkway and Path Basics

Although there is no precise distinction between a path and a walk, in general paths are narrower and less formal than walks. A 2-foot-wide walk is sufficient for one person. You may want to consider a walk width closer to 3 feet if it is the main route for

wheeled garden equipment. Make the walk a minimum of 4 feet for two people to walk side by side or to pass in opposite directions, though 5 feet is recommended. Main entrances should also be at least 4 feet wide. For wheelchair or assisted access, make walks 5 feet wide. Paths through gardens and to secondary entrances can be as narrow as 14 inches.

It is not necessary to maintain a uniform width for a path or walkway. Varying the width adds visual interest and is a way to provide space for water features, seating, potted plants, or sculpture.

If you are constructing a walk with a uniform-sized paver, lay out a section of the walk to determine the exact width. That way you will minimize cutting of the pavers.

Paths and Plants. Plan your path and adjacent plantings to minimize maintenance and to keep the path from becoming overgrown by the plants that border it. In other words, either use compact edging plants or make the path larger than you want initially so that when the plants mature, you still have the path width you want.

5

PATHS AND WALKWAYS

Opposite top: The uses you envision for your path will help determine the type of stone you select.

Opposite bottom: Wide, curving walks are an inviting way to dress up a front entry area.

Right: This stepping-stone path seems to branch off of the more formal straight walk.

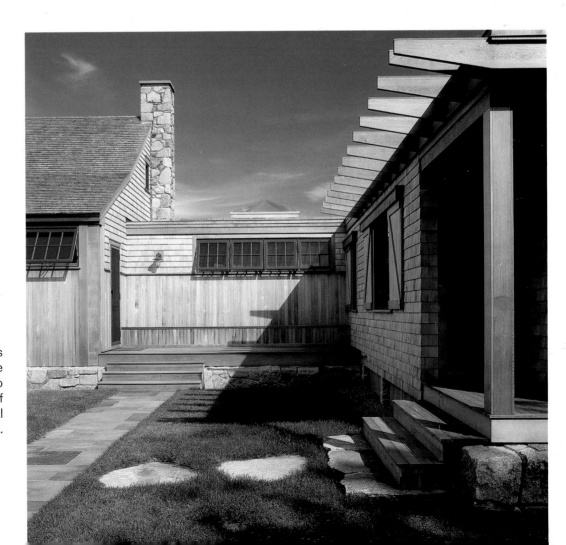

Wood Edging

Whether you use boards, squared timbers, or peeled logs for edging, choose a species that is rot resistant, such as cedar, redwood, or black locust. Do not use treated wood, recycled railroad ties, or treated telephone poles near food-producing plants.

Edging

Edging can be decorative or functional, and often it is both. For many stone path projects, it is optional.

When edging is used, it is placed along the sides of a walk to define its border and to contain loose walk materials like washed stone or crushed rock. Many landscapers and homeowners use edging to hold stonework and the sand base underneath it in place.

The edges of a walk will get displaced over time if vehicles regularly drive over it. Use substantial edging such as concrete curbs or 6×6 timbers to edge walks that cross or abut a driveway.

Edging Materials. You can use several types of materials to edge a path or walkway. Wood, collected or quarried stone, pavers, and fabricated concrete products are all suitable for edging. Plastic edging material is also available. The challenge is to choose an edging material that is functional, aesthetically pleasing, and complements the adjacent landscaping.

Edging Color. The color of the edging you select is important to the overall look of the project. Experiment with samples to see how the edging complements other features in the garden. For example, a complementary stone that was used to make a design in a walk surface might also be used to edge the drive, parking area, or beds adjacent to the walk.

Edging Height. You can install edging flush with, above, or below the level of the walk stones, or you can bury it. Each method has its advantages. Common considerations for choosing one height over another include aesthetics, what is adjacent to the walk, and the topography in the area of the walk.

Raised edging helps to contain adjacent plantings and keep soil from washing onto the walk. It can also serve as a curb to contain loose gravel or washed stone walks. Flush and recessed edging allows for water to run off easily. Continuous plastic edging is popular because it minimizes the migration of grass from lawn areas adjacent to the walk. Check the manufacturer's specifications for installing plastic edging flush with, above, or below the level of the walk stones.

Opposite: This edging maintains the informality of the walk while helping to contain the smaller stones.

Edging Options

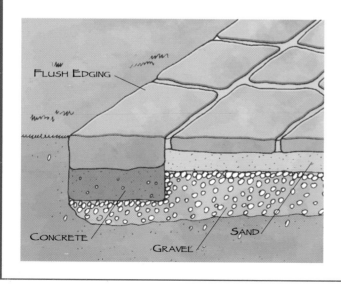

FLUSH EDGING

CONCRETE

GRAVEL

SAND

RAISED EDGING

CONCRETE

GRAVEL

SAND

6×6 EDGING

SAND

GRAVEL

REBAR

2×4 EDGING

SAND

GRAVEL

2×3 SUPPORT STAKE

Walkway Slope

Your walk can follow the natural slope of the land if the grade is less than 1 foot of rise in 10 feet of run. If it isn't, then you may want to change the grade, which will make walking on the path more comfortable. You can lengthen the walk (i.e. increase the run) by adding one or more bends. Or, you can add steps as needed to keep the grade at or less than a 1-foot-in-10 ratio. Steps can be added one or more at a time along the length of the walk, or you can construct a flight of steps wherever it makes the most sense to put them. (See "Landscape Steps," page 126.)

Gravel paths and walks need to be fairly level, otherwise hard rains and use will gradually move the gravel from the high spots to the low ones.

Drainage. On level grades, drainage is usually not a problem. But if the soil is wet, you may want to install perforated drainpipe in a gravel subbase to improve drainage. (See "Subsurface Drainage," below.)

You will also want to build up low spots to minimize flooding and puddling. This is a greater concern if your walk material is loose gravel or aggregate.

Try to avoid placing a walk across a slope where it can act like a dam and disrupt drainage patterns. If you must put a walk across a slope, install 2-inch or larger drainage pipes under the walk every 4 to 6 feet.

If a walk abuts a building, stone wall, or other garden structure, slope the walk away from the structure about ⅛ inch per foot. If the walk is 4 feet wide, the outside edge should be ½ inch lower than the edge against the wall.

Crowned Walks. Walkways made of pavers or brick are often crowned, or set so the center of the walkway is higher than the sides. Make the crown (measured from the center of the walkway to the edge) about ⅛ inch per foot. For example, a 4-foot walk is crowned ¼ inch. Flagstone walks are usually sloped across their width about ⅛ inch per foot to shed water.

Subsurface Drainage

CROWNED WALK SURFACE

EDGING

LANDSCAPE FABRIC

4" PERFORATED DRAINPIPE

2"–4" TAMPED GRAVEL

SLOPE TO CENTER.

Above: For an informal look, allow moss and grasses to grow between stones.

Opposite: To avoid ponding water, slope the path to allow for water runoff or install a drainage system.

Stepping-stone Paths

A stepping-stone path is one of the easiest stone land-scape projects to construct. Stepping-stones are typically set in lawn, ground cover, bark mulch, or gravel. They are also used in ponds for access to views, to feed fish, or as part of the path network in the landscape. Stepping-stone paths are a good choice in general for informal landscapes, but they can also work as low use or maintenance paths through more formal gardens.

Stone Selection

You can use almost any type of stone to make a path. Although stone paths are commonly made with individual stones spaced for comfortable strolling, you can use pavers laid in a pattern instead of a large single stone. Avoid using polished stone because the surface becomes extremely slippery when wet. Using stone dressed to a uniform thickness makes the work go quickly.

Laying Out the Walk

Stepping-stones can be laid singly in a line or deliberately staggered. You can also make a path that is more than one stone wide.

Before you can excavate, you need to calculate how far apart to set the stones. Fifteen inches on center is a good distance that will accommodate a leisurely stride for most people. If you want to test the path for walking comfort, walk the area where you want to put the stones and mark each spot where the center of your foot lands. Use this as a guide to set your stones. Stepping-stones used in part of a path—for example, to keep you out of a wet spot—can be set further apart, because you will instinctively change your pace when you get to the stones.

Excavate. The depth of the excavation for each stone depends on the thickness of the stone and where you want the top surface of the stone in relation to the surrounding grade. For stones set in lawn, consider placing the stone low enough to mow over. In mulch or ground cover, elevate the stone slightly above grade.

Opposite: Lay out a stepping-stone path by first taking a test walk through the yard.

Right: Here is an attractive combination of a gravel path and dressed-stone walk.

In heavy soils, excavate an additional 2 to 4 inches and backfill with gravel before setting the stones. Save or compost sod by cutting and removing it separately from the soil.

If your stones are not a uniform thickness, excavate to accommodate the thickest part of the stone. Backfill with sand to support the thinner parts of the stone.

Stones Set in Mulch. Depending on your overall design goals, you may want to excavate the entire path area, as you would for a walkway, instead of making individual holes. You would excavate the whole area if you wanted to set the stones in gravel, mulch, or a ground cover. Regardless of your method, check the bottom of the excavated areas for level before you start placing stones.

Set the Stones

After you set a stone in a hole, stand on it and check it for stability by trying to rock it. Stones that are not uniform in thickness are more likely to need fill or sand added to make them stable. Next, use a level or straightedge to see whether the top surface of the stone is at the correct elevation in relation to the surrounding grade. Repeat these steps for each stone.

Backfill. For stones set in lawn, partially backfill with the site soil and replant strips of sod, or completely backfill with soil and sown seed to allow the grass to re-establish itself. If you are planting a ground cover, you may want to use a different grade or type of soil for backfill. If you are mulching the area with gravel or mulch, you may not need or want to use any soil for backfilling.

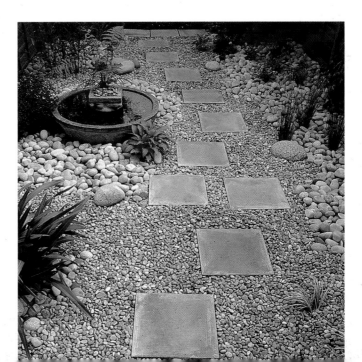

Gravel Paths and Walkways

A gravel walkway, sometimes called a soft walk, is easy and comparatively inexpensive to install. Because a gravel path can conform to any shape, they are a good choice for meandering garden paths. With a gravel walk, you won't have the heaving and displacement problems that you might have with large stones or pavers. Because gravel drains well and dries quickly, it is a good choice for garden paths. An occasional light spray with a garden hose is usually enough to wash away surface dirt.

Gravel walks do have limitations you'll want to consider before deciding to construct one. In heavy traffic areas, gravel gets pushed around and will require raking now and then to level out the surface. When compared with a hard walk surface, pushing a wheelbarrow, maneuvering a wheelchair, or walking with a walker on loose gravel will require more effort, and walking on it barefoot can be painful.

Types of Stone

Stone used for walks is usually classified by texture, either smooth or rough. Rough stones make a more compact walk surface than do smooth stones. Both are available in many colors and sizes. In the gravel path shown opposite bottom, the same smooth shaley stone that lines the lakeshore was used. This is a good example of where the material used also serves a unifying function, in this case tying the landscaped areas to the natural surroundings.

Although commercially available loose aggregate ranges from ¼- to 3-inch stones, the best sizes for paths are between ¾ and 1½ inches. These medium-size stones stay in place better than small pebbles. They compact better, too, and are more comfortable on which to walk than larger stones.

Gravel and crushed stone are typically sold either screened to a uniform size or unscreened. You can also purchase small quantities by the bag at garden centers. For large quantities, you'll want to go to a gravel yard.

Gravel-Path Construction

CROWNED GRAVEL SURFACE MATERIAL

PLASTIC EDGING

LANDSCAPE FABRIC

2" SAND

4" GRAVEL BASE

Smooth Stone. Smooth stone, sometimes called river stone, may or may not be available at a gravel yard. It is usually found at garden centers in a range of sizes and colors.

If you're unsure about the best color and size stone to use, bring home a few samples with which to experiment, and study examples in public parks and gardens.

Right: Use paths to direct foot traffic and to orient strollers to views and vistas.

Below: Using the same stone that lines the shore of the lake ties the walk to the natural surroundings.

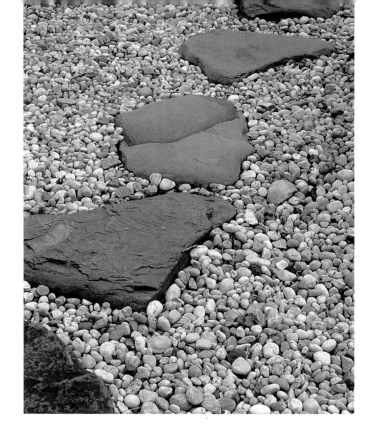

Installing a Loose-Aggregate Walk

On sites with good drainage, you can place soft walk materials in a shallow excavation without a gravel subbase. Although edging is commonly installed in trenches on each side of the walk, it is not essential. Without edging, however, some of the gravel will eventually migrate to adjacent areas. This isn't much of a concern for low-traffic paths, but you will periodically have to add new material to maintain the look of the walk.

Excavate the Site. Begin by laying out the walk with stakes and string. First, drive two 1×2 stakes at each end of the walk, positioned to indicate the edges of the walk. Then attach string to the stakes to mark the finished height of the edging. Two inches above grade is a common height for edging. Don't level the string; if the ground slopes, the string should slope with it. If the walk leads to a building entrance, make sure your lines are perpendicular to the building.

Trenches. Use a flat-bladed shovel to dig narrow trenches for the edging. Dig the trenches deep enough so that the edging just touches the string. Line the trench and the entire walk area with landscape fabric. For curved walkways, install the landscape fabric across the width of the excavation instead of running it down the length. Overlap all seams at least 6 inches. (See "Installing Walkway Edging," opposite.)

Edging. Before you begin, check your strings to make sure they are at the right height. The strings are your guide to positioning the edging and maintaining a uniform height. Use stakes to support wood edging.

For curved edging, use a rope or garden hose to create smooth curves. As you set the edging material, fill behind it with compacted soil. Bed brick or block edging by tapping the inside faces with a rubber mallet.

Spread the Loose Aggregate.

Add the walk gravel in 1-inch layers, spreading and tamping each layer until the material is ¼ to ¾ inch from the top of the edging. The walk surface should be at or above the surrounding grade. You can slightly crown the middle of the walk to improve drainage.

Construction Tip

Plotting Curves

Lay out curves with two ropes or garden hoses. Outline one side of the curve with a rope or hose. Use sticks cut to the appropriate length to set the width of the walk. Place them at intervals as shown. If your walk is not a uniform width, you can use the same layout technique with different-length sticks to indicate the varying widths of the walk. Outline the other edge of the walk with the second rope or hose. Sprinkle flour or sand or use marking paint to outline the excavation area.

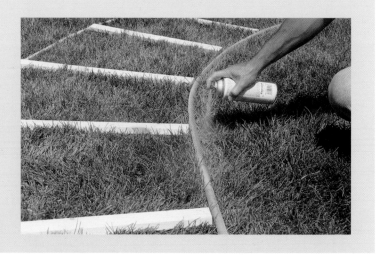

Opposite: Install loose aggregate in 1-in. layers, tamping between layers to avoid settling later.

Below: Seldom-used garden paths like this do not require edging, but you may need to replenish the stone periodically.

Installing Walkway Edging

EDGING

LANDSCAPE FABRIC

MIN. 6" OVERLAP

FABRIC FOLDED INTO EDGING TRENCH

GUIDELINE

Dry-Laid Flagstone Walks

A dry-laid flagstone walk is set on a gravel and sand base. Properly installed, it will last more than a lifetime with little maintenance. Though the following instructions are for working with flagstone, you can follow the same steps to install brick, Belgian block, or concrete pavers for a walk.

Walk Design

Begin by determining the exact width of the walk. If you are using rectangular pieces of stone in one or more sizes, do a trial layout of several courses on a hard, flat surface, like a driveway. Include the spaces for joints in your layout.

Ideally, you want a walk that is the correct width without creating the need to cut stones. If you are working with irregularly shaped pieces of flagstone, you can skip this step because some cutting will be necessary. However, the more you plan, the less cutting and shaping you will need to do.

Left: A curving flagstone walk doubles as a border for a planting bed.

Opposite: A walk of irregularly-shaped flagstones leads to a playhouse and arbor.

Dry-Laid Flagstone Path Construction

FLAGSTONE

2" SAND   4" GRAVEL

LANDSCAPE FABRIC

Lay Out the Walk. Establish the outline of the walk as described in "Excavate the Site," page 98. To shed water, the walk should slope side to side about ⅛ inch per foot. Mark one stake at each end of the low side of the walk to establish the walk's height. Typically, this is about 1 inch above ground level. Use a level to transfer this mark to the other two stakes. From this mark, measure up the appropriate distance to establish the correct slope. Then set your strings to indicate the finished height of the walk.

Mark the Ground. Mark the location of the walk edges on the ground by sprinkling flour or sand over the strings or using surveyor's marking paint. Make sure your string location marks are clear, and remove the strings to excavate the area. You will reattach the strings later.

Excavate the Site. Use a pickax and shovel to excavate an area about 1 foot wider than the finished walk size. This will give you room for forms and edging material (optional). The excavation needs to be deep enough for 4 inches of gravel (more in a wet site), 2 inches of sand, and the thickness of the paving material. If your soil is gravelly and drains well, you may be able to omit some or all of the gravel. Once the edges of the walk are excavated to the approximate depth, reinstall the strings so that you can use them to check for the correct depth. Once the area is excavated, use a tamper to compact the subsoil. Install landscape fabric in the bottom and up the sides of the excavation.

Lay Stone in Sand

Spread about 2 inches of gravel in the excavation; tamp it; level it with a rake; and tamp it again. Continue to add gravel until the top of the form board set on the gravel is level with the strings.

Set Forms. Drive 2×3 stakes at the ends of the excavation and every 2 to 3 feet along it. Position the stakes to allow for a 2-by form board with the inside face in line with the string that marks the edge of the walk. The forms hold the edging in place and serve as a guide for a screed. Attach the form boards to the stakes with screws.

If the sides of your walk abut a planting bed and the overall landscaping design is informal, you can eyeball the edges or intentionally make them irregular. In this case, the forms are there to screed the sand.

Above: Use a notched 2x6 or a 2x4 attached to a longer board as shown to screed the sand level.

Below: Set the flagstone by placing each stone in position and tapping with a rubber mallet.

Spread the Sand. Shovel builder's sand evenly over the compacted gravel, and spread it with a rake. Thoroughly dampen the sand with a gentle spray. Fill in and dampen any low spots. Repeat the process, building up the sand so that the paving material will be ¼ to ½ inch higher than the intended walk height to allow for settling.

Screed the Sand. While the sand is moist, pull a notched 1×6 screed board in a zigzag motion along the form boards to level high spots and fill in low spots in the sand bed. After screeding, dampen the sand again with a fine mist.

Set the Paving Material. Working from one corner against an edging or string, place the stone in the desired pattern and spacing without disturbing the sand bed. Joints in irregular flagging will vary, but try to keep them consistent within a range: ½ to 1 inch works well for most applications. Trim irregular flagstone as needed to fit.

If you are laying a pattern in courses, mark the walk layout on the forms and stretch a string across the marks to maintain the courses. Check for level frequently. Remove any stones that don't conform or aren't stable, adding or removing sand as necessary. Tap each stone into place with a rubber mallet. If you are working with small-dimension stone, lay several square feet and then place a 1×6 straddling several stones and tap it with the mallet. Repeat until all the stones have been set.

Avoid standing or kneeling directly on the sand bed or freshly laid paving. Place a piece of ½-inch plywood over the paving before you stand or kneel on it. Or prepare the sand bed, and lay the stone in small sections.

Below: If plants will form the border of your walk, remove the forms and backfill with soil or mulch.

Fill the Joints. To fill the joints with sand, spread a thin layer of mason's sand over several square feet of the paving. Use a stiff broom to sweep the sand into the joints. Sweep in all directions. Add more sand as needed to fill all the joints. Sweep excess sand into a pile and remove. Lightly spray the walk with water to pack the sand down and to wash it off the surface. Allow the surface to dry; then repeat the process until all the joints are completely filled in and compacted.

Remove the Forms

When the walk is complete, carefully pull up the temporary forms and shovel gravel along the outside of the walk or edging and behind the landscape fabric. After tamping, finish backfilling with a few inches of soil, decorative stone, or mulch.

Over time the joints may need to be refilled. If a stone heaves or settles, remove it. Re-form and water the sand bed; replace the stone; and refill the joints.

Above: For an informal walk that goes through a garden, use wide joints and irregularly-shaped stones

Stepping-stones in Water

You can use stepping-stones into or through a shallow pond or stream to make a path layout that works best for your landscape. Steps through water also give you vantage points that you wouldn't have from shore. For formal gardens, use square or rectangular cast-concrete slabs, large quarry tiles, or cut stone for path stones in water. In a less formal setting, you can use irregularly shaped rocks or flagstones. In either case, you will have to decide on an arrangement for the path stones. As a rule, a random or zigzag pattern is more interesting than stones set in a straight line. Choose stones that are large enough and spaced close enough—12 to 15 inches between stones—for a comfortable walking stride.

Setting the Stones. There are several ways to set stepping-stones in water. The variables are: the depth of the water, the size of the stones, and whether or not there is liner material on the bottom of the water feature. In all cases, it is crucial that once the stones are set, they are completely stable. The first step to assuring stability is setting the stones on undisturbed or well-compacted soil.

You can set large stones with flat bottoms directly into the water. If the stone cannot be set securely without rocking, then you may need to make a nest of concrete to cradle the stone.

If you've installed a flexible liner or preformed shell for a water feature, you will have to take additional precautions to set stepping-stones without tearing the liner. For very large stones, you may need to install a concrete footing under the liner material if the soil is not well compacted. You will also want to sandwich a piece of liner material between the stones and the liner to protect the liner.

Adding Piers. In deeper water, you will need to build a pier for each stone. Piers are most easily made out of concrete, brick, or cut stone. Generally, they will need a poured concrete footing for support and stability. Make the footing at least 3 inches larger than the pier on all sides.

Safety Considerations. Set stepping-stones high enough above the water so that the walk surface stays dry. Wet rocks are often slippery, and if they're constantly wet, algae or moss can grow on them making them even more slippery. For that reason, avoid placing stepping-stones near waterfalls or fountains. Porous rock such as sandstone is more prone to develop moss than nonporous rock such as granite. Check the steps regularly for any slick buildup, and scrub it off with a stiff brush. Walk across the stepping-stones from both directions on a regular basis to check for shifting or movement that makes the stones rock unpredictably. Over time you may occasionally have to reset stones that become unstable.

Left: Large slabs of quarried stone form a bridge across this pond. Note the support where the slabs meet.

Opposite: Set stepping-stones above water level to help keep them as dry as possible.

Stepping-stone Options

Brick with Cap **Boulder** **Fieldstone**

NOTE: A STABLE CONCRETE FOOTING SHOULD BE PLACED UNDER EACH TYPE.

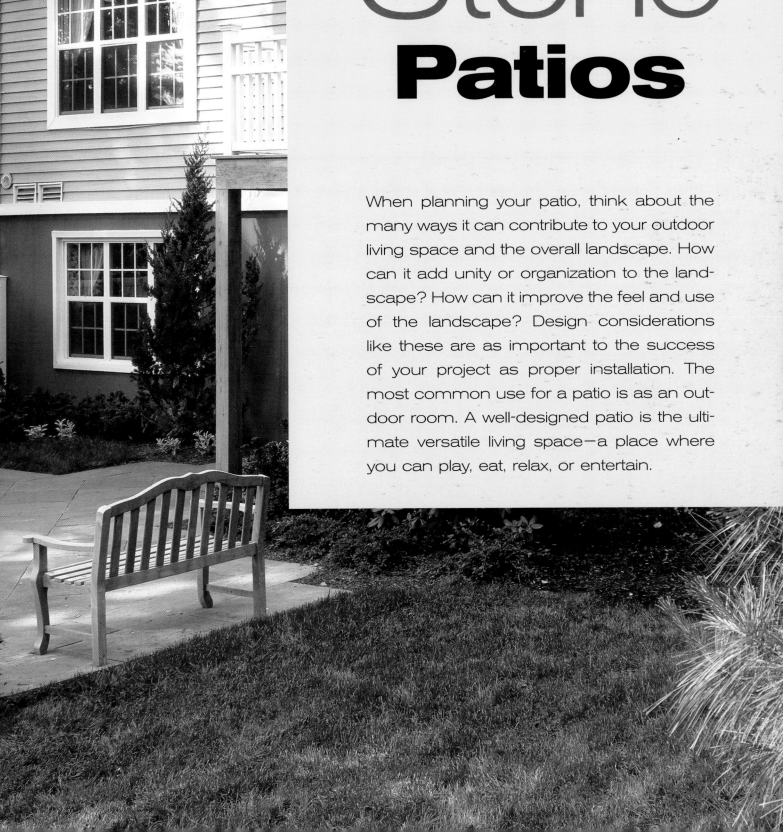

CHAPTER 6

Stone
Patios

When planning your patio, think about the many ways it can contribute to your outdoor living space and the overall landscape. How can it add unity or organization to the landscape? How can it improve the feel and use of the landscape? Design considerations like these are as important to the success of your project as proper installation. The most common use for a patio is as an outdoor room. A well-designed patio is the ultimate versatile living space—a place where you can play, eat, relax, or entertain.

Patio Uses

Patios make inviting outdoor living areas, but they can also serve other functions. The patio shown in the photo opposite bottom is an example. From the patio you can step up onto the veranda, or you can take the stepping-stones that lead to two other house entrances. From the opposite side of the patio you can reach stone steps that take you to a lower garden. In other words, its location helps to organize the entire backyard area. Even the shape of the patio makes a significant contribution: it adds an architectural complement to the house, and it helps tie a nearby S-shaped stone wall to the rest of the landscape.

Building a patio is not difficult as long as you pay attention to the details and complete each step before you begin the next. The patio installation techniques described and illustrated here are versatile: with them you can build durable hard surfaces to use as entryways or courtyards, or even to create a secluded spot away from the house.

Installing a Dry-Laid Patio

Installation techniques for a dry-laid patio are essentially the same no matter which type of stone, pattern, shape, or size you choose. But natural stone that is not dressed to a uniform thickness takes more time to install than uniform pieces because you need to adjust the depth of the sand bed to accommodate the thickest stones. Crazy paving, made of irregularly shaped pieces, and intricate designs also take longer to install than rectangular stones.

As a general rule, a professional spends about half the installation time on preparation and half on setting the stone. The amount of preparation time increases if you excavate by hand, move gravel and sand without a bucket loader, or use a hand-held tamper to compact the gravel.

Tool Suggestions. A masonry saw makes it possible for you to consider building a patio with a complex design, so you might consider renting one. If you do plan a complex design, work it out on paper and

Dry-Laid Patio Construction

1½" COARSE SAND

THIN LAYER FINE SAND

4"–6" GRAVEL

LANDSCAPE FABRIC

TREATED-WOOD EDGING

FLAGSTONE

make templates for the various shapes. Cut all the stone at once and make a few extra of each shape for spares. During construction, you can use a masonry blade in a circular saw to make cuts. You can also use a chisel and hammer to cut the stone, but this gives the stone a different type of edge.

Above: By varying the width of a walkway, you can create a seating area. The walkway leads to other entrances of the house.

Below: A pattern such as the one shown here adds architectural interest and becomes a focal point in the overall landscape design.

Grading Basics

To prepare a slope or uneven ground for a patio or walkway, remove the sod and topsoil by hand; for larger areas use a backhoe or bulldozer. Level the subsoil by cutting and adding fill. Bring the grade up to the desired elevation by adding new fill and compacting it to a uniform depth over the entire area. Resist the temptation to add new fill only; this is not a stable base for a patio. For stability you need layers of similar types of soil to minimize shifting, sliding, and heaving over time.

Layout. Begin laying out your patio by marking the corners with stakes. If the shape is irregular, place a rope on the ground to mark the outline. Use layout paint to draw the shape on the ground. (Layout paint is available at building supply stores.) Chalk, lime, and cornstarch also work for outlining but are difficult to use if it's windy and less permanent.

Above: Add a gazebo or other type of structure to help make a patio more inviting.

Building a Patio

To mark the perimeter of a rectangular patio, construct batter boards about 1 foot outside the footprint. If one side of the patio is adjacent to a structure, drive two stakes next to the building so that strings attached to them accurately indicate the edges of the patio. Use mason's or carpenter's twine or a substitute that does not stretch. Check rectangular patios for square. Don't assume the adjacent building is square.

If it won't complicate any future construction projects, square the patio to the adjacent wall. If a building is out of square and the patio goes around a corner or is adjacent to an inside corner, you may have to modify the paving pattern.

Mark the corners on the ground. Use a plumb bob, and mark each corner with a painted or flagged spike. To transfer the footprint to the ground, stretch strings between the flagged spikes near the ground. Use these lines as a guide to paint or lime the patio footprint on the ground.

Checking for Square

Here's a method that ensures corners are square: mark one string tied to a batter board 3 feet from the corner; mark the other string 4 feet from the corner; and measure the distance between the marks. If it is 5 feet, the corner is square. It it isn't, adjust the string until the distance is correct.

Opposite: A seating area off of the main patio allows the owners to take advantage of the stunning views.

Above: Get a sense of the true size of your planned patio by laying out its borders with string.

Right: Combine patio pavers of varying sizes, shapes, and colors for an interesting effect.

Leveling

The easiest way to establish level is to set up leveling lines inside the perimeter. It is possible to use the perimeter squaring lines to establish level, but because this can be confusing, it's not a good way to start. Use 1×2 or larger stakes. If the shape of the patio is irregular, set the strings near the edges of the footprint. Level the strings with the most accurate leveling tool you have. (See "Leveling Tools," page 72.) Make a permanent mark on each stake to indicate the location of the line for level. Check the location of the leveling lines before using them: lines inevitably get bumped and tripped over during construction, and animals can also displace them.

Right: Adjust strings attached to stakes to provide ⅛ in. of slope per foot of patio.

Opposite: Is this patio encroaching on the lawn, or is the lawn encroaching on the patio?

Above: Use bricks as patio borders or to create frames for quarried stone.

Below: This ground-level patio and elevated porch provide a multilevel outdoor living area. The same type of stone covers the patio and steps.

Calculate the Slope

Patios must have at least ⅛ inch per foot of slope to drain satisfactorily. On a circular or irregularly shaped patio, the slope can be pitched in different directions. Large patios can be pitched in two opposite directions to minimize the change in elevation from one side to the other. In any case, pitch the slope away from structures and travel paths. Consider the patio's size and shape, the elevation of adjacent thresholds, and the location of the drainage channels. Then establish the slope in whichever way makes the most sense.

Establishing Slope. To establish the slope, you will need to adjust the leveling strings. For example, if a patio is 14 feet wide, the slope from one side to the other will be at least 1¾ inches. Depending on the existing grade, you can establish the slope several ways. You can slide the string up 1¾ inches on the side nearest the house, drop the level 1¾ inches on the side farthest from the house, or make up the 1¾ inches by taking a little from one side and adding a bit to the other. For example, you could raise one end 1 inch and lower the other end ¾ of an inch. To help maintain the slope during construction, place additional leveling strings perpendicular to the main leveling lines.

Using a Story Pole

Because most patios are near a house entrance, it's important to learn how to make and use a story pole that includes the elevation of the threshold in relation to the top surface of the patio stones.

To make a story pole for sites that require less than 4 feet of new fill, use a 5-foot-long 1x2. Square one end. Beginning at the squared end, make a mark to indicate each layer of fill and stone needed above the leveled subsoil. For example, you could allow 6 inches of gravel for drainage, 2 inches of sand, and 2 inches for the stone paving. This total is the elevation for the edge of the patio nearest the house. Mark the board 1 to 3 inches above the top of the paving mark to indicate the location of the threshold.

To estimate excavation and fill needs, begin by removing the sod and topsoil. Set the story pole at the edge of the area where the planned patio will be nearest the house. Place a level between the point below the threshold where the top surface of the patio will be to the story pole. Stretch a line or use a board if the distance is more than the length of your level. Check to see how the actual reading compares with the mark on the story pole for the finished top surface. If the reading is above the mark on the story pole, raise the grade; if it is below, excavate. Repeat this process wherever there are grade changes within the area for the patio. In addition to the existing grade variables, the far side of the patio should be lower than the edge nearest the house, at a rate of at least ⅛ inch per foot.

STORY
POLE

DOOR

THRESHOLD

FOUNDATION

TOP OF
THRESHOLD

TOP OF
STONE
1"–3"
BELOW
THRESHOLD

FIELDSTONE

2" SAND

6" GRAVEL

COMPACTED
SOIL

LANDSCAPE FABRIC

Excavate the Soil

The excavation area for the patio includes its footprint and 6 to 12 inches beyond the footprint on all sides, except where the patio abuts a building or an existing paved surface. Remove any plants or sod within this area. Use the sod to patch lawn elsewhere, or compost it. Dig out the topsoil, and reserve it for grading.

Use a Story Pole. A story pole can help you visualize and estimate excavation and fill needs when you are preparing a level area at a particular eleva-

tion. It can also help you see potentially awkward grade changes at the edges of a patio. Having this information early on in a project can help you incorporate grade changes into your landscaping plan.

Excavation Depth. Before you can calculate the excavation depth you need to answer two questions: What is the total thickness of the patio, and where do you want the finished surface of the patio in relation to the adjacent grade? For example, 1½ inches of stone, plus a 2-inch sand bed, plus 6 inches of compacted gravel equals a total patio thickness of 9½ inches. If you want the finished surface to be an inch above the adjacent grade, you will need to excavate a depth of 9½ inches minus 1 inch, or 8½ inches.

Right: Even patios with informal designs should have slopes that allows water to drain away from the house or paved surfaces.

Below: Using small stones in the manner shown here is a labor intensive process, but the results are truly unique.

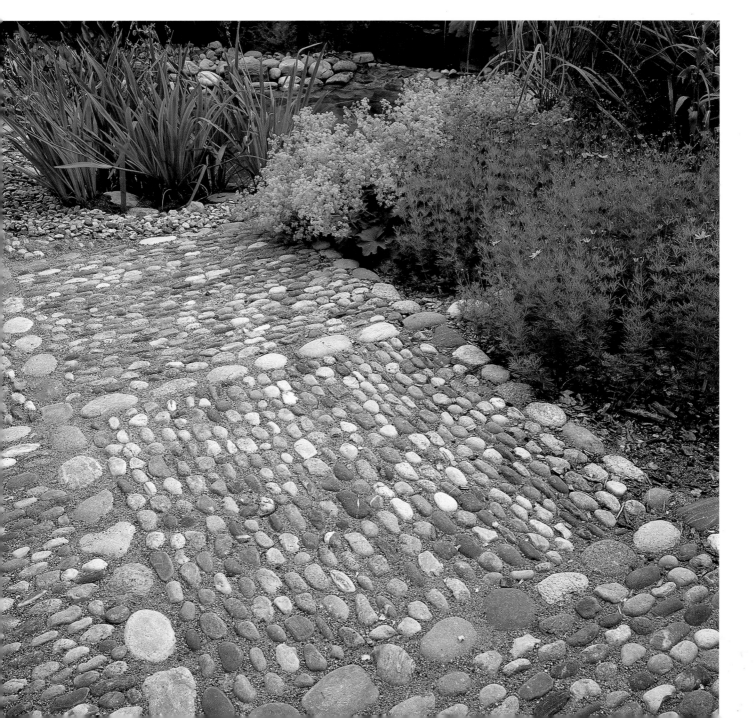

Cold Climate Drainage

In heavy soil or unprotected locations that experience temperatures below 0° F, you may need a gravel base that is up to 12 inches thick. Ask a local landscaper to recommend a gravel thickness for severe site conditions.

Above: Embed pipes in the sand. Pull a 2x4 across the pipes to level the sand bed.

Use your sloped leveling lines and a story pole to excavate or fill the entire area to a uniform depth with on-site subsoil.

Tamp the fill each time you add 2 inches of material. Consider renting a power tamper for large areas or if you have to add a lot of fill. You can compact up to 4 inches of material at one time with a power tamper.

Lay weed barrier fabric over the graded subsoil, overlapping the joints about 6 inches. The fabric suppresses unwanted vegetation and, more importantly, keeps the subsoil from migrating into the gravel. Soil can clog gravel, restricting its drainage capacity.

Add a Gravel Base

If you are tamping the gravel by hand, lay it in 2-inch layers. If you are using a power tamper, lay it in 4-inch layers. Use sloped leveling lines to spread the gravel to a uniform depth at the desired slope.

Add a Sand Bed

You can use coarse cement sand or fine mortar sand for the sand bed. Or use a combination as shown in the illustration on page 108. Lay two 1½ to 2-inch diameter pipes on the gravel bed about 4 feet apart. Pull a 2×4 over the pipes to spread the sand to a uniform depth. Maintain the same slope as the gravel.

After leveling one area, reposition the pipes and repeat step one. Fill the spaces that the pipes left with sand, and level to match the grade on either side. Check the entire bed for slope with the leveling lines or a level. Add sand to bring the grade up to the desired elevation. After the sand is in place, re-establish the perimeter of the patio on the sand with layout paint or string.

Opposite: A flagstone patio appears to blend into the surrounding vegetation.

Above: Fill the joints in a sand-base patio with sand, or allow moss or grass to grow in the joints.

Right: Create continuity in your landscape by using the same or similar materials on different elements throughout the yard.

Make Tamping Easy

Smart Tip

When using a hand-held tamper, let the tool do the work to get the most uniform compaction. Don't force or twist the tamper in an attempt to further compact the gravel.

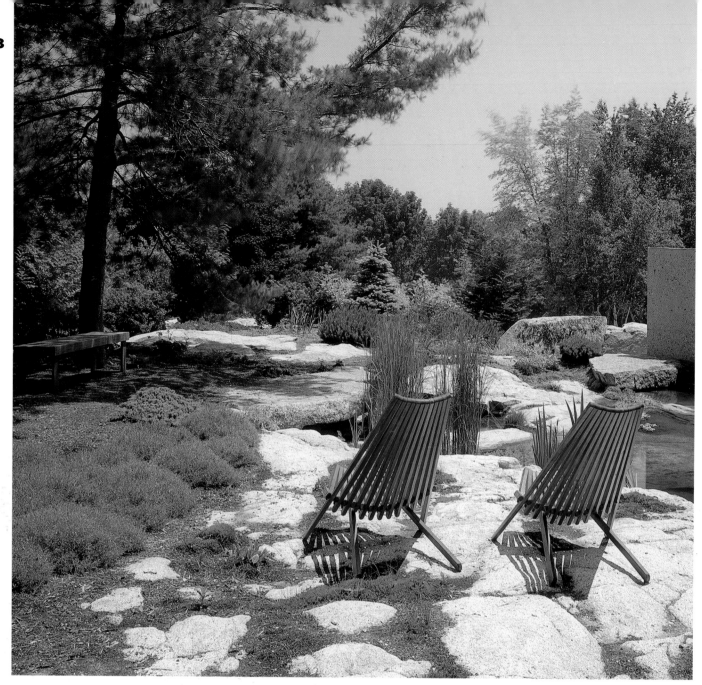

Plan Carefully

If you plan to plant a ground cover between the stones of a patio, think about the ratio of stone to vegetation you want. Many ground covers grow out over the stones, hiding parts of them and making the planting area look larger than planned. If you don't want this look, you have several options. You can opt to not plant in all of the spaces between stones; or you can make narrower planting spaces, use larger stones, or choose a ground cover, such as thyme, that is easy to trim.

Above: Sometimes a natural outcropping of stones can serve as a ready-made sitting area.

To Edge or Not

Edging is optional. It can act as a guide during instal-lation, as a barrier to vegetation, or as a decorative touch. If you install it as a guide, you'll set it below the finished surface and eventually cover it with soil, grass, or washed stone. You can also set it flush to or slightly below or above the finished surface of the patio. There are numerous edging options, but firm earth is the best choice if there is any chance that frost will heave the edging.

Choose a Pattern and Spacing

A stone pattern can do more than please the eye. It can direct traffic flow, define the edges of the patio, or break up the patio surface to define areas according to their uses. Patterns can also ease a potentially awkward transition.

Experiment with your stone to decide on a pattern and joint size. The joint size for crazy paving often varies from ½ inch to as much as 2 inches, for example. You can lay uniformly shaped pieces as tightly as possible—¹⁄₁₆- to ⅛-inch—or space them farther apart. Use spacers to maintain a consistent width between stones. Spacers are available from tile and masonry suppliers, or you can make wooden ones out of scrap lumber. Make homemade spacers the width of your joints and the depth of the stone, plus at least ½ inch for easy removal.

Above: Patios made of small-dimension stones will usually require a border to keep the material in place. This planting bed serves as part of the border.

Right: Irregularly sized joints will give your patio a casual look. Joints of all the same size lend a formal look.

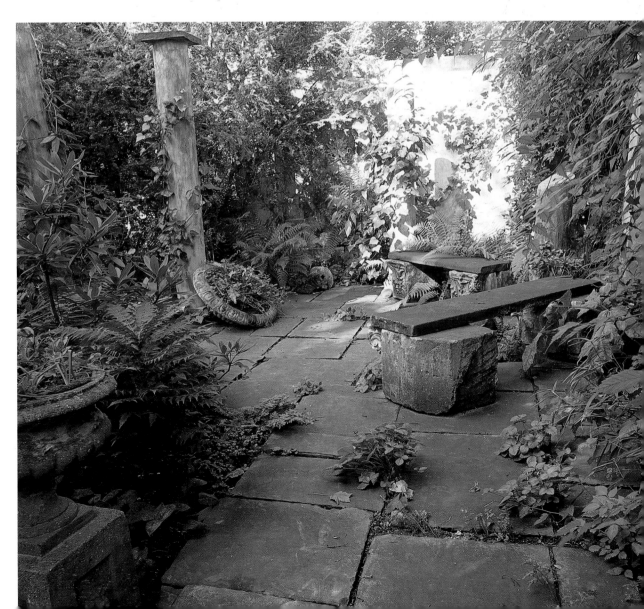

Design Tip

Formal or Not?

Before you begin laying stone, decide whether or not you want an irregular edge. You can trim the stones along the patio edge to meet the perimeter line or leave them uncut and irregular. An irregular edge is less formal and easier to install, and it makes an attractive transition to a planting bed or border.

Set the Stone

Both the shape of the patio and the pattern of the stonework determine the place to begin laying the stone. The usual location is at a corner or along one edge, but some designs are best started from a center point.

To set a stone, place it on the sand bed and strike it several times with a rubber mallet. Uniform support from the sand bed is critical to keeping the stone from breaking. The larger the pieces, the more important it is to support them completely. If you have any doubt about how a stone is set, lift it and inspect the impression in the sand. Add sand wherever the stone did not touch the sand bed.

Use your leveling lines and a level to check your work as you proceed. If you use stones that vary in thickness, check your work frequently for level.

Left: Combining different materials with stones of varying shapes and sizes leads to unique designs.

Above: Finding an exposed outcropping or ledge provides you with an instant patio.

Opposite top: The curve in this patio helps create a natural-looking transition to the wooded area.

Opposite bottom: You might use gravel as a filler, especially when there are large joints between stones.

Fill the Joints

After all the stones are laid, fill the spaces between them. Sand and soil are the most commonly used materials to fill joints.

Sand Fill. Use fine mortar sand, which is angular rather than round, to fill the joints. Angular sand compacts well and is disturbed less by foot traffic. Use a broom to push the sand into small joints. To fill larger joints, use a small spade or a bucket. Water gently to compact the sand. Refill the joints as needed to compensate for settling and displacement.

Soil Fill. Use soil to fill the joints if you want to grow a ground cover between the stones. Choose a weed-free soil mix that contains appropriate nutrients. The ground cover will become established quickly without competition from weed seedlings.

Mortared Patios

Many people prefer mortared patios because they have a formal look and provide total weed control. But consider this decision carefully. Mortared patios have some downsides, too. They are more expensive to build because they require a concrete foundation. You will either need to build a slab foundation or have a concrete contractor build one for you. Or you can use an existing concrete surface as a foundation if it is clean, intact, and at least 3 inches thick. Secondly, mortared patios do not flex. Thoroughly evaluate the potential for heaving before deciding to mortar patio stones. Replacing broken stones or repairing sections of a mortared patio heaved up by frost or tree roots can be difficult.

Choose and Dry Fit the Stone

You can use almost any kind of stone to make a mortared patio as long as it doesn't break easily or crumble at the edges. Stone that is fairly uniform in thickness is the easiest to work with and requires less bedding mortar than irregularly shaped pieces.

It is important to keep the foundation clean and to remove dirt and dust from the stone while you are working. The clean surfaces will strengthen the bond between the stone and the mortar. If you use irregularly shaped flagging, test fit all the stones before mixing the mortar. Trim and shape the stones to maintain the desired joint width. If there are joints in the foundation, arrange your stones to avoid placing a patio joint over a joint in the slab.

If you have prearranged your stones on the patio, begin by removing the stones in a 4- to 6-square-foot area. If you are using porous stones that can wick moisture out of the mortar, wet them thoroughly before beginning work.

Opposite: A mortared patio with crisp, neat joints lends a formal look to any landscape design. Using stones of different sizes can soften the overall look.

Mortared Patio Construction

MORTAR

FLAGSTONE

1½" MORTAR BED

CONCRETE BONDER

4" CONCRETE SLAB

4" GRAVEL

Calculating Mortar Requirements

To calculate the amount of bedding mortar you need, multiply the patio dimensions by the thickness of the bed. Divide this number by 12 to get cubic feet. Divide the number of cubic feet by 27 to get cubic yards. For example, a patio 24 feet long x 20 feet wide x 1.5 inches thick equals 720. Divided by 12, it equals 60 cubic feet. Divided by 27, it equals 2.2 cubic yards.

To estimate the amount of mortar you need for the joints, calculate the volume as a percentage of the total patio. For example, a 20-foot x 24-foot patio is 480 square feet. If the joints are 1 inch wide and the stones are 2 feet square, the amount of mortar needed will be $\frac{1}{12}$ of 480 (calculate the mortar on two sides of each stone—in this case 2 inches for 2 feet or $\frac{1}{12}$), or 40 square feet. 40 square feet x 1.5 inches equals 60. Divinding 60 by 12 equals 5 cubic feet, less than $\frac{1}{5}$ of a cubic yard.

Another method to calculate the amount of mortar you need for joints is to fill the joints in an area, say 4 x 4 feet, and see how much you use. Then multiply that amount by the number of 4 x 4-foot areas remaining.

9

STONE PATIOS

Use a Bonding Agent. Before spreading the mortar on the foundation, paint on a bonding agent according to the manufacturer's instructions. Bonding agents improve the bond between the foundation and the bedding mortar. The better the bond, the less likely it is that a section of mortar bed or stone can pop loose from frost or heaving.

Lay the Mortar. Mix the mortar as described in "Mortared Stonework," page 78. Begin laying the mortar bed at an edge or a corner. Spread the mortar uniformly to a depth of 1½ inches thick in 4- to 6-square-foot areas at a time. Use the edge of your trowel to make furrows in the mortar.

Set the Stone. Wipe off any excess water from each stone as you use it. Set a stone on the mortar bed, and tap it several times with a rubber mallet to set it in place. Check for slope and elevation. Add or remove mortar, or use a shim stone to maintain the slope and elevation. The finished mortar bed should be no less than 1 inch thick. As you work, remove mortar from the surface of the stones with a damp cloth. Repeat this process until all the stones are set. Wait 24 hours before grouting the joints.

Grout the Joints. You can purchase prepared grout in colors or mix your own using one part portland cement to two parts mortar sand. Mix and add water as you did for the bedding mortar. Use a mar-

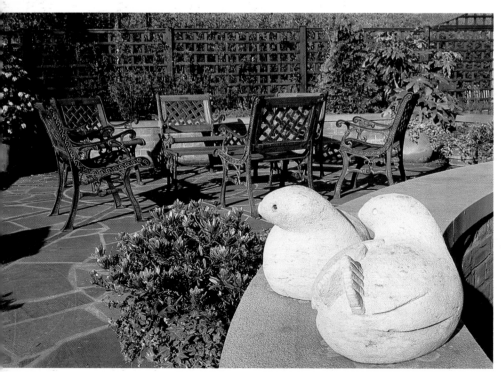

Left: Tool joints for a neat appearance once the mortar has had a chance to set up.

Above: Stone works well in most landscapes. Here, a flagstone patio and walkways tie different areas of this yard together.

Opposite: When setting stone in mortar, be sure to remove mortar from the face of the stone before it sets. Wipe from the center of the stone toward the joints.

Opposite far right: Stone provides a waterproof surface for displaying container plants.

gin trowel, another small trowel, or a mortar bag to fill the joints. Compress the mortar, and fill the joints again so that they are flush with the top of the adjacent stones.

Tool the Joints. When the mortar holds the imprint of your thumb, you can tool the joints. Compact and shape them with a trowel, an appropriately sized piece of pipe, or a jointing tool.

Clean Up. Rub excess grout from the stones with a dry cloth 5 or 6 hours after grouting. Following that, wipe the stone clean with a damp cloth, wiping from the center of the stones toward the joints. Do not wipe over the joints.

Curing. The long-term strength of mortar is dependent on slow curing. Keep the surface of the patio wet for 3 to 5 days. If you can, sprinkle it with water, and cover it with a sheet of plastic during this time.

6

STONE PATIOS

CHAPTER 7

Landscape
Steps

Stone steps come in all sizes. Depending on your choice of materials and the building site, they can be simple or time consuming to build. Stairs made with individual stepping-stones are the simplest to build and are adaptable to a range of garden styles. More challenging are such projects as setting large 5-inch-thick granite treads or mortaring flagstone to a concrete staircase—projects appropriate for formal gardens and entrances. Choose the type of project that best suits your needs.

Step Design

Some people add steps to their landscape because they simply like the way they look, not out of necessity. If your slope is less than 10 percent, that is, it rises less than 1 foot in 10 feet of run, then steps are optional. However, one or more single steps can add texture and interest along a gently sloping path.

All types of steps have a few design considerations in common.

Rise and Run

The surface on which you stand when you walk on stairs is called the *tread*. The height or distance from the top of one tread to the top of the next is called the *unit rise*. It is the relationship between the depth of the tread (*unit run*) and the height of the unit rise that makes steps more or less comfortable to use. Typically, the taller the unit rise the shallower the tread. As a rule of thumb for exterior steps, the combined length of one tread and two risers should be 25 to 27 inches.

Step Layout

Common Tread/Riser Relationships

11"~13"
7"

12"~14"
6½"

13"~15"
6"

14"~16"
5½"

Rise and Run

Run

Rise

Above: Deep treads are common in landscape steps. They encourage people to stop and enjoy the view.

Opposite top: These stairs make it easy to reach the plants on the hillside.

Opposite bottom: Stairs made of dressed stone add a touch of formality to this garden.

Similarly, a recommended range for the rise be-tween any two steps is 5 to 7 inches. This gives you a tread depth of between 15 and 17 inches. Many land-scape designers favor a 15-inch run and 6-inch rise for garden steps.

Finding the Rise and Run. Before you can make a decision about the unit rise and run, you need to calculate the total rise and run for the stairs. Rise refers to the vertical distance from the bottom of the first step to the top of the top step. Run refers to the horizontal distance from the front of the lowest step to the back of the top step.

To calculate these distances, drive a short stake at the point at which you want the top of the steps to start, and use a tall stake to indicate the front edge of the bottom step. Attach a string at ground level to the bottom of the short stake; stretch it taut; and tie it to the tall stake. Use a line level to level the string. Mea-sure the distance from the string to the ground at the tall stake: this distance equals the total rise—the com-bined height of each step. To find the run, measure the distance between the stakes. (See "Step Layout," opposite.)

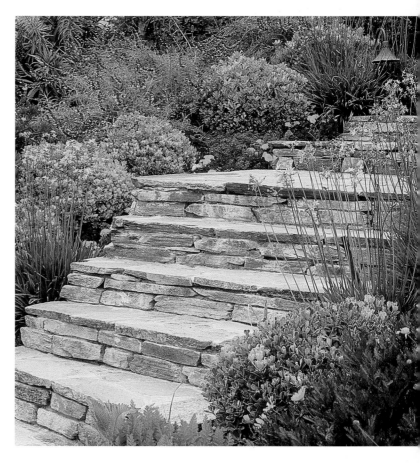

Construction Tip

Altering the Run

H ere are ways to alter the run of your steps.

- At the bottom or top of the stairs, slope and landscape the adjacent grade to fit a more comfortable unit run/unit rise ratio in the space you have.
- Add a landing part way up the steps.
- Add bends or curves to the steps to lengthen the run.
- Build a stone landing at the bottom of the steps that has a rise that is different from the rise of the first step.
- Make the top tread deeper.

Left: Each of these steps is actually a large landing, which is acceptable for landscape steps.

Above: Ground covers allowed to spread along the risers add an interesting design touch.

Opposite top: These steps may not be necessary, but they add texture and interest to the area.

Opposite bottom: This unusual combination teams individual stone risers with gravel treads.

Calculate Unit Rise and Run

Once you know the total rise and run, you can figure out the unit rise and run. To determine the unit rise, divide the total rise by the potential number of steps. If your answer is lesser or greater than 5 to 7 inches, you may want to adjust the number of steps. For example, if the total rise is 38 inches and you have five steps in mind, you'd have a riser height of 7.6 inches. But six steps will give you a unit rise of 6.3 inches ($38 \div 6 = 6.3$), well within the ideal range for outdoor steps.

Tread Depth. Now use your unit rise dimension to calculate the tread depth, or unit run. Using the measurements 1 tread + 2 risers = 25 to 27 inches as a guide, in our example, twice the unit rise is 12.6. If you subtract that from 25 and 27 you end up with treads somewhere between 12.4 and 14.4 inches deep.

Now multiply the depth of the treads by the number of steps. Does it equal the total run? Most likely it will not. When your initial rise and run combination doesn't fit into the ideal range, make adjustments to design steps that are safe and comfortable to use. As a safety precaution, maintain the same riser height for all the steps in a flight. For tips on making adjustments, see "Altering the Run," opposite.

Steps through a Wall

Laying up steps as you would short sections of retainer wall is one way to build wide steps without having to use large stones and excavation equipment. This style of step is commonly used to make steps through a wall. The top tread can be made out of one or more stones. Using dressed stone for the tread gives a more formal appearance, but the uniform surface is a desirable feature, especially in high-traffic areas.

Step Width

In addition to aesthetic considerations, think about how you will use the steps. If they are in a garden where you often walk along with another person, you may want steps at least 5 feet wide. Four feet is a generous width for one person. In a less formal garden, stone steps as narrow as 16 inches may be adequate. The layout and construction is basically the same regardless of the size of the stones you use.

The way the steps fit in with the scale of the surroundings is another important consideration in choosing a step width. For example, steps from a large patio would be wider than steps adjacent to a smaller patio. Steps leading away from high traffic areas are generally smaller than those used as a main entrance.

"Steps through a Wall," above, shows how to make wide steps without having to handle massive individual stones. Many people prefer steps constructed from large stones because of their dramatic design qualities. If you have your heart set on steps made from individual large stones, you will need equipment and an operator to move them into place. If you want to set the stones yourself, you may be able to rent a small bobcat locally. You can also set moderately large stones with a 40-horsepower or larger tractor and bucket.

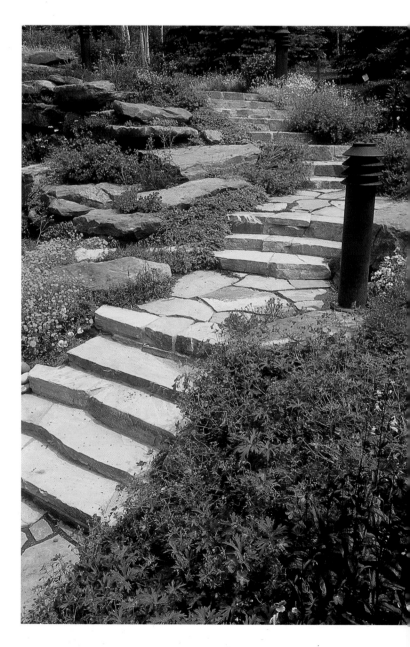

Right: Adding landings to your steps makes the climb more comfortable, and they provide a way to adjust the rise-and-tread relationship.

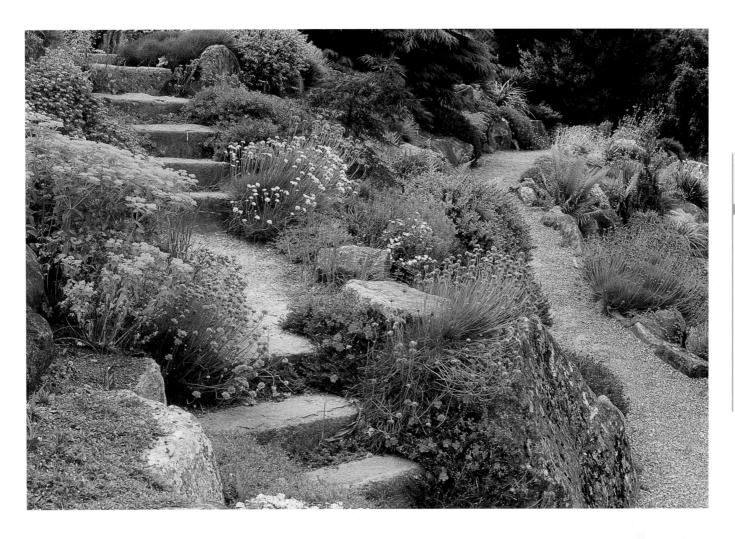

Above: Narrow garden steps complement this informal hillside rock garden.

Right: Consider combining materials for steps. Here landscape ties and gravel work together to form steps.

Below: Place large individual stones on a firm base; add well-draining gravel if necessary.

Building Steps

After you decide on the size and number of steps, cut and fill the area where the steps will go. The process is similar to cutting and filling for terraced walls. As with most stone projects, the quality of the soil where the stone rests is just as important as the stone itself. Undisturbed, well-drained soils are best for building steps. In all other soils, excavate an additional 4 to 12 inches and backfill with gravel that packs and drains.

Below: Spend time setting the first step; it will provide the foundation for the next steps.

Opposite: Short walls in a terraced yard provide ready-made steps. Add plants to the terraces for impact.

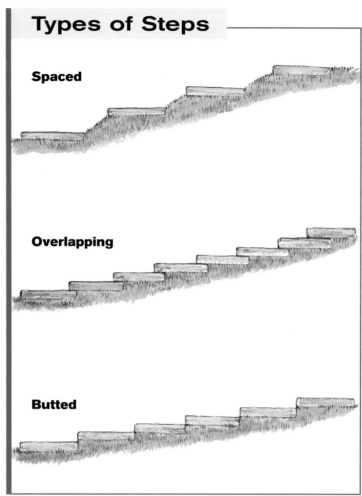

Types of Steps

Spaced

Overlapping

Butted

The First Step. There are three basic ways to set step stones: overlapped, butted, and spaced. Begin at the bottom of the flight, using one of the following ways. The secret to landscaping stone steps is to make sure that the first step is set securely. A good first step provides a firm foundation for the second step and so forth. Follow these guidelines.

• The front edge of the first tread may rest on the hard surface of a patio or walkway.

• Excavate and set a base stone that is level with or slightly above the adjacent grade.

• Remove the topsoil; replace it with gravel, sand, or stone; and set your first step on it. Add 4 to 6 inches of gravel—more if you are building on slow-draining soil.

• Create a landing area with a different rise than the rise between steps.

Built-Up Step Construction

INTERIOR FILL STONES

COMPACTED SOIL

IRREGULAR INNER FACE

SQUARE OUTER FACE

TREAD CAP STONE

COVERED JOINT

4"–6" GRAVEL

FOOTING STONE

7

LANDSCAPE STEPS

Using Undressed Stone

If you use fieldstone or undressed quarry stone for landscape steps, adjust the depth of your excavation so that the rise between the steps remains constant.

Set the Remaining Steps. Once the first step is set, continue setting the steps, using a mallet to firmly bed each stone. Check your work to maintain the same rise between the steps.

Inspect the steps after a hard rain, and make adjustments if a step rocks when you step on it. In climates with freezing temperatures, inspect steps each spring for dislodged stones.

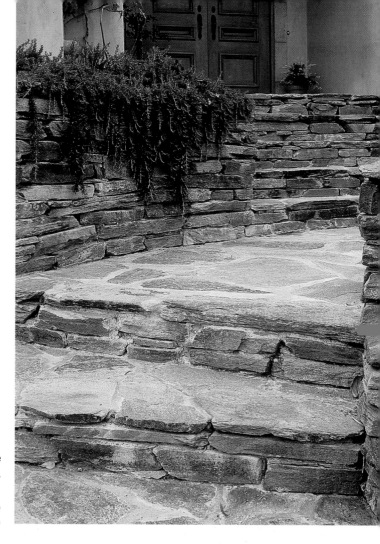

Right: Mortared steps require a concrete base. Include the thickness of the mortar bed in rise/run calculations.

Below: If you are using large treads of dressed stone, adjust the width of the stair to eliminate cutting.

Mortared Steps

Steps made with mortared flagging or pavers require a concrete foundation. However, before you can install the foundation, you must know the thickness of the stone in order to calculate the rise and run of the foundation. Add 1 to 1½ inches for mortar to your calculations.

If you use pavers, adjust your dimensions to use full-size pavers. If you use random-sized flagging, test-fit the stones before mixing the mortar.

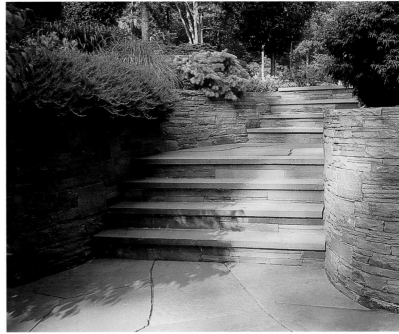

Left: Inspect steps each spring for damage that may have occurred over the winter. Look for loose stones.

Above: Steps, patios, and walls made from the same type of stone create a unified design.

Below: This unique design consists of wood dividers that separate blue small-dimension stone.

CHAPTER 8

Stone & Water
Features

Combining water and stone in landscape design has been popular for millennia. Even a small amount of water in the landscape can have a large impact on the overall design. While the importance of water features in the landscape varies from person to person, the life-giving property of water is undeniable and affects how the viewer perceives the overall landscape design. Although your local climate will influence composition and formality, you can integrate this revered combination into any landscape.

Carving a Water Bowl

A stone water bowl provides a sculptural feature adaptable to any type of garden. You can use one as a prominent focal point or tuck one in an unexpected place for surprise, texture, or as part of a smaller composition within a larger landscape. Whether polished, rough, geometric, or freeform, a bowl of water rewards the viewer with visual enticement created by the play of light, shadow, depth, and reflection.

Carving a water bowl need not take a lot of time. There is no need to buy expensive specialized tools—though renting certain professional-grade tools will make the work go along more quickly.

However, creating a polished surface on the bowl does require sophisticated equipment. If you want this look, consider carving out the bowl yourself and having a stone sculptor polish it.

Left: Pump kits make fountains, waterfalls, and other features possible in the landscape.

Below: The natural markings on this stone add depth and texture to the bowl.

Opposite left: A masonry basin filled with found stones makes an interesting feature.

Opposite right: Water bowls can have a rough-hewn look or be highly polished.

Water Features

Small water features are relatively inexpensive and easy to install, yet they can have a big impact on the landscape. You can install water bowls and low-flow, gravity-fed fountains and other features virtually anywhere. Water features that rely on pumps also provide an environment for water-loving plants that would otherwise be impossible to maintain.

Circulating pump kits available at home centers and garden centers make the installation of water features such as streams, ponds, and waterfalls relatively straightforward. Some kits offer the opportunity to combine features, such as a pond with a fountain or a waterfall with a stream.

Find Your Stone

Some types of stone are easier to carve than other types. A stone with distinct layers is not recommended for carving because it tends to split and break up too easily. Sandstone and limestone are softer and require less muscle to carve than metamorphic rock, such as marble. A more homogeneous stone presents fewer carving challenges in terms of predictability, hence the popularity of marble for carving.

Natural Indentations. Natural or blasted rock that already has an indentation will reduce the amount of time it will take to carve out a basin shape. If you have a circular saw with a masonry blade, a right-angle grinder, and a few good chisels (and your arms are up to the task), you can carve out a 12-inch-diameter by 5-inch-deep basin in an afternoon.

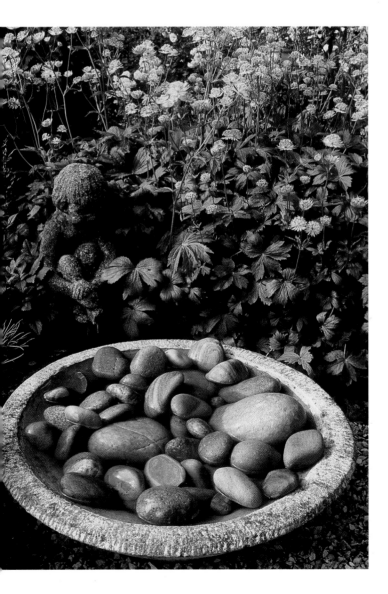

Examine the Stone

Examine your stone for fractures, and note their location in relation to where you will carve out the basin. To check for fractures, thoroughly wet the stone and let it air dry. Fractures will show up as wet lines after the overall surface of the stone has dried. The presence of fractures does present an increased risk of having the stone break apart while you are working on it. But you can still use it. For best results, carve out small pieces of stone, and calculate the direction and impact as you carve to minimize stress on a fracture line. When shopping for stone, ask about local stone that is less likely to fracture.

Even if your stone has no obvious fractures on the outer surface, it may have some hidden ones. As you carve, frequently examine the area where you are working for fractures. An attentive work habit will more likely result in a finished bowl instead of a pile of rubble.

Choosing a Chisel and Hammer

Use a pointed chisel if the stone is soft. For working hard stone, a 1-inch blunt or flat chisel is a good all-purpose size. If your chisel does not have a carbide edge, sharpen it often as you work. If you are unsure about the hardness of your stone and the type of chisel to use, experiment with both. After a little practice, it will become obvious which one to use.

A 2- or 2½-pound sledgehammer is a typical size for this kind of carving. Hammer technology has changed significantly in the last 10 years, so it may make sense to shop for a new one for your carving project. In general, any tool that works for concrete will work well on soft stone.

Rough-out the Bowl

Outline the shape for the top rim of the basin with a nail, graphite, chalk, or a felt tip marker. Holding the chisel at about a 45-degree angle, make a ¼- to ½-inch-deep groove along the outline. **1**

Cut in Sections. Cut pie-shaped sections no more than every 1½ inches using a circular saw with a masonry blade or a chisel and hammer. The smaller you make the pie sections, the easier it is to even out the surface of the basin. Also, the larger the piece you try to remove, the less control you have.

Starting at the rim of the bowl, place your chisel in one of the cuts and hit the opposite end of the chisel with the hammer to remove pieces of stone. Work

Carving the Bowl

1 Cut pie-shaped wedges using a circular saw with masonry blade, or hammer and chisel.

2 Use the hammer and chisel to remove small sections of stone. Work on small sections to maintain control.

3 You have the option of leaving the surface rough or using a grinder to achieve a smoother surface.

Opposite: Place water bowls so that people in the garden come upon them unexpectedly.

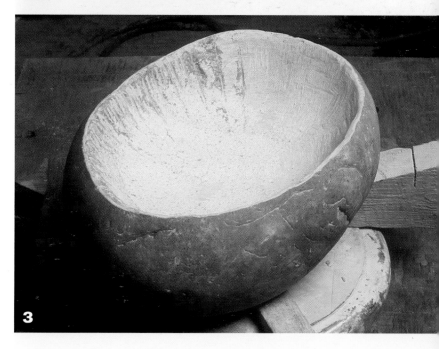

your way around the rim of the basin; then gradually work toward the center. **2** After you have removed all the stone to the depth of the cuts, again divide the area to be carved into pie-shaped sections and carve out (pitch) the stone you want to remove. Continue in this manner until the bowl is roughly the depth and shape you want.

Finishing the Bowl

After the bowl is roughed out, continue to remove stone in smaller pieces to smooth out the surface. **3** At some point, you will have to decide how smooth you want the surface to be, and what kind of lip or edge you want the bowl to have. The bowl shown in the photos on this page has a crisp edge determined by the original layout. You can round this edge to varying degrees by working it down with your chisel and hammer. You can tool and finish the surface of your bowl in a number of ways, from rough to highly polished. The tools you have available to you and the type of stone with which you're working will determine in part how you finish the bowl.

To achieve a softer, less angular finish, smooth out the surface with a low-grit grinding wheel attachment on a right-angle grinder. (Consider renting a heavy duty professional-grade grinder for large projects.) Soft stone can be worked wet, which keeps the stone dust to a minimum, or dry.

Smart Tip

Working When Wet

If you opt to work with an electric grinder on wet stone, plug the tool into a ground-fault circuit-interrupter (GFCI) outlet. All outdoor outlets are required to be equipped with GFCI protection. These types of outlets can cut power to the circuit if there is a grounding fault. If you don't have one handy to your work area, you can get an adapter for a regular electrical outlet.

Maintaining the Water Bowl

Because the water in a bowl is stagnant, you will need to change it occasionally. If unwanted moss or lichen grow on the bowl, remove it with a brush. No soap is needed. Use a soft-bristled brush on soft stone.

In climates with below-freezing temperatures, empty water bowls in the fall to reduce the risk of fracturing the stone from freezing water. Tip the bowl upside down; cover it with a tarp; or cover the basin with a piece of plywood to keep out snow and rain.

Constructing a Fountain

Stone fountains come in all sizes, from a dinner-plate-size basin to a prominent garden feature 4 feet or more across. You can install these fountains in a lawn, in a flower bed, or on a terrace or courtyard. Fountains are popular additions to sitting areas, and for centuries they have been installed near house entrances in hot, dry climates.

Fountain Types. Because the reservoir is buried, a recirculating water feature that resembles a bubbling spring is a good choice for households with small children. A boulder or pebble fountain is easy to assemble and is adaptable to any landscape aesthetic. They can contribute both moisture and a cooling effect in the area immediately surrounding the fountain. If you have access to electricity, you can install this type of fountain wherever you can excavate a hole large enough for a 5-gallon pail. You can also create the reservoir from a broader, shallower container with a similar volume or form a basin made of flexible pond liner material.

Stone for the Fountain

Stone yards often stock large, predrilled boulders for fountains, or they will custom drill to your specifications. There are many variations of the boulder fountain, including boulders with a basin carved out, a stone bowl, or a basin with a hole drilled in it and tooled sculptural pieces of stone. An old millstone or an arrangement of stones can also be used with the hardware for a boulder fountain.

Smooth, worn stones, sometimes called river stone, are typically used for pebble fountains.

Left: Pond kits make this type of design feature possible. Experiment with shape and sculpture.

Right: For safety's sake, bury the reservoir for a small spring or fountain.

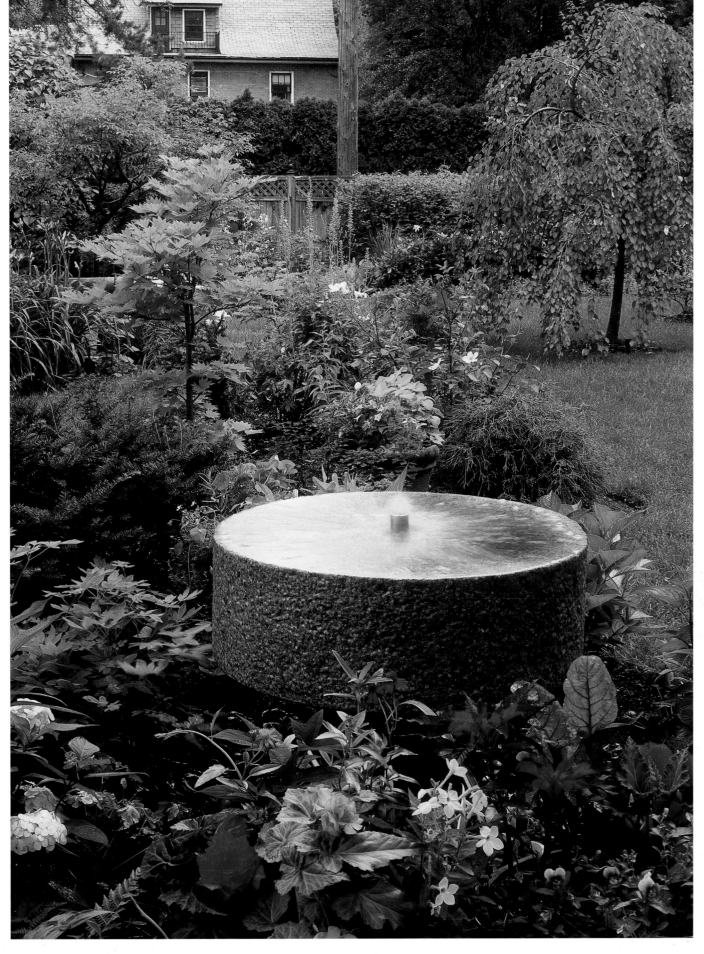

Above: Some stone yards will drill through stones for fountains and other water features.

Pump Assembly

Vertical gusher spouts or bubblers are usually used with fountain-style water features. They can be adjusted from 3 to 24 inches or higher depending on the size pump you use. If you have questions about matching the size of the pump to the fountain, discuss the project with the fountain supplier. As with any fountain, you need to have easy access to an electrical outlet with GFCI protection.

Installing the Pump

Begin the installation by digging a hole slightly larger than your reservoir. (See "Fountain Construction" opposite.) A 5-gallon plastic pail works well as a reservoir. Place the reservoir into the hole, and check to make sure it is plumb. Backfill the hole with soil, and contour the soil at grade level to create a basin that will funnel the water back to the reservoir.

Set the fountain assembly in the reservoir, and drill a hole in the side of the pail near the top for the electrical cord. Place a rectangle of flexible liner material (pond liner or heavy plastic sheeting) over the reservoir, pushing the material down slightly into the pail. The liner material should extend far enough beyond the edge of the reservoir to serve as the catch area to return the water to the reservoir. Use scissors or a knife to cut an 8- to 10-inch X-shaped hole in the liner centered over the reservoir.

Place a piece of wire mesh (at least 10 inches larger than the diameter of the reservoir) over the liner. Cut a hole in the mesh large enough for the vertical pipe that connects to the fountain pump. For pebble fountains, trim the pipe if needed so that the stones will hide it. Test the assembly by filling the reservoir with water and following the instructions in the fountain kit to adjust the flow of water.

Fountain Construction

WIRE MESH

FLEXIBLE LINER

SMOOTH STONES

DISCHARGE PIPE

RESERVOIR

FILTER

SUBMERSIBLE PUMP

Fountain Maintenance

The amount of water your fountain will lose to evaporation will depend on how often you run the fountain and the ambient temperature. Using a stick, check the level of the reservoir frequently until you can establish a refilling schedule.

Algae. You can remove algae that builds up on the fountain stones by scrubbing them with a soft-bristled brush.

Freezing. Empty the reservoir before freezing temperatures can turn the water to ice. Check the reservoir if you have a mid-winter thaw or rain. Remove any water that accumulates from groundwater runoff.

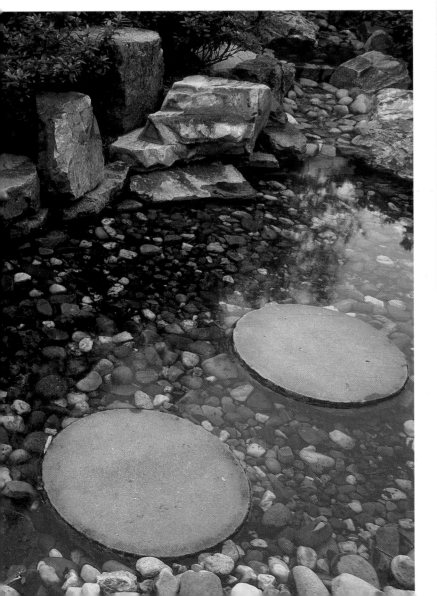

Opposite: A bubble fountain is combined with a larger water feature.

Left: Stepping-stones provide a dry path across a shallow pond.

Above: Small stones mimic a stream that flows from a small fountain.

Bends in the River

Use bends in a streambed to draw the eye to other garden features, such as a specimen plant or a viewing spot with seating.

Dry Streambeds

A dry streambed is a desirable garden feature that provides visual interest and often serves more than one function. It can create space to display favorite plants, provide a solution to a difficult grade change, disguise a drainage channel, and of course, create the illusion of water where it is impractical to install a water feature.

Design

A dry streambed mimics nature, so let nature be your guide in designing one. Notice how rocks in or adjacent to a stream are dispersed when the water moves at different speeds, and when the terrain is steep or level. Experiment with stones of different sizes and shapes and their placement. Although some trial and error is inevitable, place your stones and plants with both nature and your design goals in mind to achieve the most naturalistic results.

Installation

Stone in a dry streambed has three uses: it forms the edge or bank of the stream; it takes the place of water; or it makes the streambed itself. Usually, stone for a dry streambed is used 'as is' and is less expensive than wall or patio stone.

Any changes you make after the initial installation can usually be done with hand tools. In fact, you can install many dry streambeds with a shovel, pry bar, and wheelbarrow. Low-tech installation and relatively inexpensive materials make a dry streambed an ideal project for a homeowner with little do-it-yourself experience.

Installation Savvy

- Use hose or a rope to lay out the shape of the streambed you desire.
- Use a plastic barrier under the streambed for weed control.
- Set large boulders and rocks first.
- Cover any areas that are not planted at the time of construction with plastic and mulch until you are ready to plant. This will reduce erosion and control weeds.

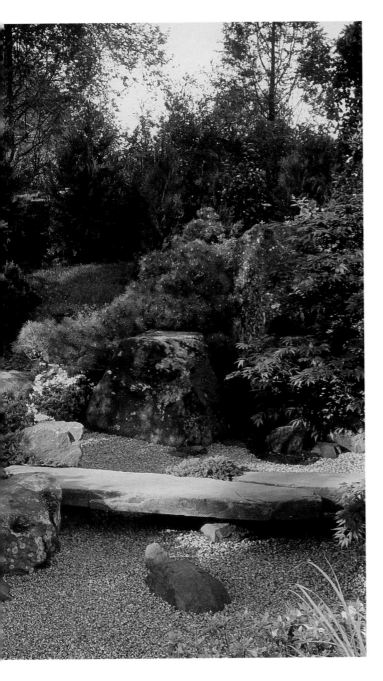

Opposite: Place pavers to create bridges or stepping-stones over a dry streambed.

Left: Vary the width of a dry streambed to add visual interest to the design.

Above: Stones can mimic a number of natural features, such as beaches, rapids, or falls.

The Natural Look

The following design guidelines will help you construct a natural-looking dry streambed:

- Choose a layout that fits the topography and natural drainage patterns of the site.
- Change the character of the streambed if it goes through different parts of the garden. For example, use larger angular stones on a steep grade to indicate a falls.
- Vary the width of the bed. Add a beach or dry pond for visual interest.
- Vary the depth and steepness of the banks for visual interest and to enhance plantings.
- Make islands of vegetation or stone.
- Place stepping-stones or a bridge across the streambed.
- Use shadows from nearby foliage plants to mimic rippling water.

CHAPTER 9

Setting Large
Stones

Nowhere is the popularity of landscaping with stone more evident than in the increasing use of large stone. You can use large stone to imply or intentionally mimic natural formations, create a mood, convey a message, or construct functional garden features. At the same time, their shapes and mass add dramatic texture, beauty, and character to the landscape. With greater access to earthmoving equipment, cranes, and bobcats, homeowners can now consider landscaping with large stones.

Explore the Possibilities

In the project shown at right, a hole was blasted in ledge for part of the house's foundation. Much of the stone came out of the ground in ½- to 2-ton pieces. The stone's wealth of color, texture, and shape appealed to the homeowners and greatly influenced their landscaping plans.

Their primary landscape goal was to feature, not hide, the fact that the house was built on top of ledge. All the functional elements, such as the entrance walk, drive, retainer walls, and grade changes, were constructed with this goal in mind. Native plants were used extensively to complement and enhance the wooded, rocky site.

Creating Focal Points. When planning your project, bear in mind that large stones are focal points within a landscape. In a strong composition, there is also a dynamic relationship between the stones in a grouping. As a designer, you want to figure out how to build those relationships into a visually pleasing whole and tie the composition to the surrounding landscape.

Trying to re-create nature is the most challenging kind of project you can attempt with large stone. The more natural you want the stone to look, the more carefully and intentionally you must place it. A thoughtless placement will look like one forever.

Stone and Other Features. When a composition is part of an obvious constructed element, such as a walkway or entrance, it is a focal point much like a piece of sculpture. You want it to fit in terms of scale, color, shape, and surface quality, but your emphasis is on a visually engaging feature, not necessarily a natural one. Which is not to say that you ignore

the fact that you are working with a natural material. Successful installations, even obviously constructed ones, contain some natural essence of the stone—how it ages, breaks up, lines a streambed, forms a mountain—something that is authentic and recognizable as true about stone in nature.

Incorporating the size, shape, and surface qualities of your stone is as important as the precise location and angle of each stone. In addition to the design information in Chapter 1, use the following information to test and develop your ideas for a composition using large stone.

Construction Tip

Burying Stone

When you work with large stones, you often bury one-third or more of each stone. Dig test holes on the site early on in the planning stage, and before you buy stone, to make sure your site can accommodate your design. If your soil is shallow, sometimes you can substitute flat-bottomed stones, provided you can make them stable and secure.

Left: The stone the owners found when blasting for the foundation of the house influenced their landscape plans.

Below left: Consider combining stone with plantings and man-made features.

Below: The availability of heavy equipment makes the use of large stones in the landscape possible.

Basic Shapes

The strongest defining characteristic of stone is its shape. Hence, the shapes of the stones you use make a valuable contribution to your composition. If the composition is only viewed from a distance, then you will rely even more on shape to make the composition effective.

Natural stone has varying degrees of rounded or angular edges and can be grouped into one of six basic shapes. The following descriptions of stone shapes refer to the appearance of the stone after it is installed, or its effective shape. When you select stone, you must consider how much of it will be buried and how that will alter its shape.

Vertical or Upright

Vertical stones appear distinctly taller than they do wide. They are often used to catch or direct the viewer's eye, to help frame the composition, or to add 'backbone,' emphasis, or strength. Using several vertical stones can easily create a border or boundary. A single medium to large vertical stone, particularly one with an unusual surface, is highly sculptural and can evoke serenity and strength.

Horizontal

Three basic stone shapes fit under the general heading of horizontal. For the sake of discussion, they are identified as large, low, and wedge.

Large horizontal stone is unmistakably wider than it is tall and is often dominant in a composition. Large horizontal stone with angular edges is a good choice for a rugged dramatic waterfall, or to create a natural-looking rocky outcrop. Using rounded stone gives a warmer, aged feel to an installation. In the featured project (pages 152–153), several large horizontal stones are used to make a gradual grade change on one side of the house.

Low horizontal stone can be a smaller version of large horizontal stone, or it can be very low flat-topped stone most often used for steps or edging. In a composition, low horizontal stone is less dominant than larger stone, whether it is horizontal or vertical. Nevertheless, one or more can be integral components that contribute depth, balance, detail, and fullness to an installation.

Wedge-shaped stone can be any size and typically has a rounded worn surface that evokes restfulness or tranquility. Its distinguishing characteristic is an obvious slope or incline that is prominently featured in the composition.

Stone Shapes

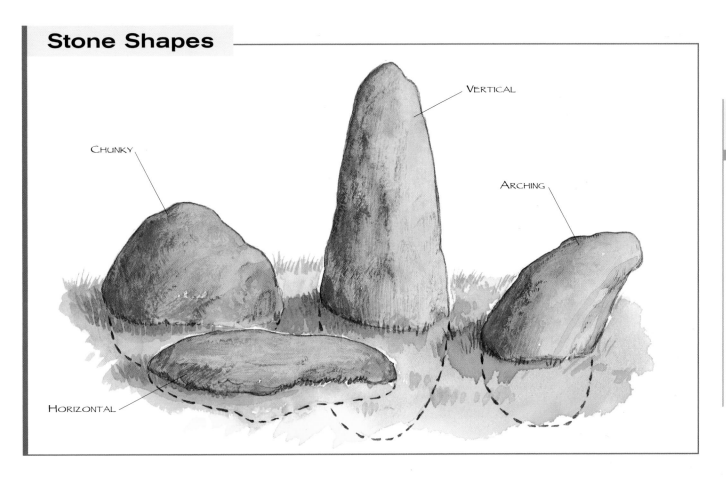

CHUNKY

VERTICAL

ARCHING

HORIZONTAL

Opposite: Blocky and horizontal stones are combined in a landscape design.

Right: Low-profile horizontal stones balance the sections of a seating area.

Blocky or Chunky Stone

Blocky or chunky stone is used in all sizes. It is cube-like in form, though more often slightly taller than wide. This is a versatile shape with which to work and is a strong presence in a composition. You can use it peripherally or as a central component to add depth, cohesion, density, and stability to a composition.

Arching

Arching stone is less common and for that reason needs to be used with the utmost care to be integrated into a composition. Arching stone has a distinctive bend that strongly conveys movement, direction, or energy. It is distinctly longer in one direction than the other and can be oriented vertically or horizontally. In a composition, arching stone can easily lead the viewer's eye to a focal point or can direct foot traffic.

Surface Qualities

The surface quality of stone varies widely. The degree of roundness or angularity of the edges is the most pronounced surface quality. Other common surface qualities are fracture lines or fissures, pitting, and distinctive layers. Since stone is not homogeneous, there may be variations in surface quality when a stone is made up of more than one type of rock. In the Northeast for example, whitish streaks of quartz are commonly found in stone.

In a composition, use surface qualities to engage the viewer and contribute authenticity, unity, or logic. As an example, consider the 'lines' that are created by the layers in sedimentary stone. If you set these stones with the 'lines' going off in all directions, the composition will have a chaotic quality. Perhaps it would appear whimsical or playful, which is fine if that's the effect you want. However, this arrangement would not work if you were trying to mimic a natural formation, because in nature the striations in a given type of stone go in the same direction. The above example also illustrates that surface quality can contribute to the mood the composition is designed to evoke.

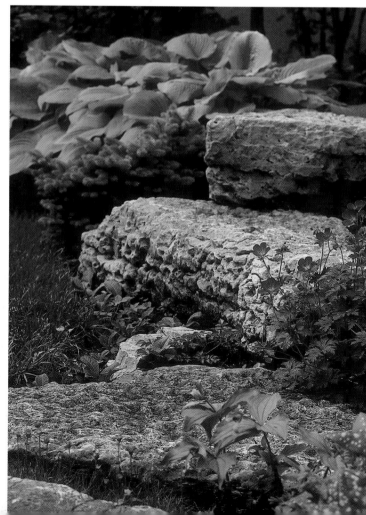

Above: Take surface characteristics into consideration when arranging stone in the landscape.

Top right: Using a variety of stone shapes helps create an interesting composition.

Right: To create a natural look, plan and experiment with the placement of the stones.

Opposite top: A line of striking stones forms a pathway across an open field.

Opposite bottom: A flowering shrub forms the backdrop for a simple arrangement of stones.

Using Large Stones

You can arrange large stones to serve a practical function, resemble or imply a natural form, evoke a mood or movement, or convey a message or information. Below are some examples for each of these uses of large stone.

Natural Forms
Island
Peninsula
Mountains / Hills
Streambed
Waterfall
Trees / Flowers
Fish, Dragons, Birds

Functional—Actual or Implied
Bridge
Gate
Border
Retaining Wall
Step
Dam

Mood or Movement
Flowing or Swimming
Awakening
Harmony
Humor
Illusion
Strength
Tranquility
Stillness
Permanence
Eternity
Family

Message or Information
Ruins
Guardian or Protector
Ceremony
Beckoning or Welcoming
Sculpture
Boundary
Direction

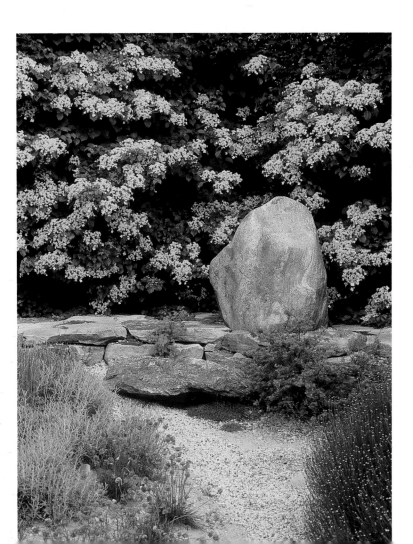

Creating an Arrangement

Nuances of placement are just as important as understanding how the qualities of the stone itself contribute to your composition. The placement of the stone and the quantity you use also affect the mood or tone of the composition. Will it be grand, sparse, energetic, or tranquil? Once you have a mood or tone in mind, you must somehow integrate it with the degree of naturalness you want the composition to have.

Rely on Experience. While arranging large stone may be a new endeavor, you can draw on your experience in arranging and decorating rooms to guide you through the process. The key considerations include combining large and small components, color, orientation, spacing, texture, form, elevations, framing, light, and views from different angles.

Ultimately you want to create a strong composition that has both a defining character and a distinct relationship to the surrounding environment. Judicious use of ratios, spacing, orientation, quantity, and companion plantings will help you achieve that goal.

Ratios

Ratios can help you determine the sizes of the stones you'll need to create a pleasing composition. If a composition has seven stones, assign the largest one a value of 100 percent. Two or three may be 65–75 percent of that; two or three others would be 30–45 percent of the largest stone; and one or two more would be 15–20 percent of it. Ratios are not absolute, but they serve as a sizing aid to use when you select stone for a composition. They yield the most information when used with other design tools, such as spacing and orientation.

Spacing

The amount of space between stones within a composition contributes to its wholeness or internal unity. Attention to spacing is also essential to create dynamic relationships between individual stones in the composition.

If stones are placed too far apart, they lose their connection to one another. If they're too close, their individual character is diminished. These guidelines hold true for purely sculptural compositions and for compositions that suggest or mimic natural features. In the latter, the care with which you space the stone also contributes to the authenticity of the composition. It should look like a grouping you might find in nature.

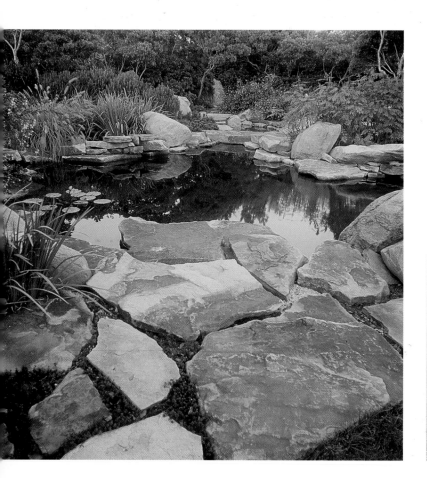

Left: Use stones of various sizes to create a unified composition.

Below: Add design interest by combining large stones with smaller ones in a grouping.

Opposite: Interior decorating experience can provide landscaping ideas.

Use Props. Spacing stone is a trial-and-error process that you can partially work out using a scale model or full-size cardboard shapes on the site. Large stone is cumbersome and expensive to move around, so make as many spacing decisions as you can before the actual installation.

Orientation

As with spacing, orientation deals with the position of stones in relation to one another and with the overall integrity of the composition. To make decisions about orientation, evaluate what the faces and shape of each stone can contribute to the composition from all possible views. You may also play with the tilt or angle at which the stone is set.

Quantity

At some point during construction, you will have to make a decision about how many stones to use in a composition. Using 20 to 40 percent stone in a landscape is a general guide for projects of any scale. On the other hand, a Japanese-influenced composition could be 90 percent stone.

General recommendations are helpful, but it's still a challenge to know when to stop, even for a professional landscaper. Give yourself time for deliberation. Sometimes it can be helpful to add stones you're not sure about and then take them out later. Less is more if the composition seems complete with fewer stones. An odd number of stones is almost always easier to arrange than an even number.

Companion Plantings

If plants are part of your composition, include them in the plan drawings right from the start. This will help you avoid the disappointment of an arrangement with insufficient or too much space for plants. If you plan the space for plants at or near their mature size, you will minimize the amount of pruning needed to maintain the desired proportions of plant and stone.

If certain plants are essential to the overall composition, know the characteristics of the plants you choose for the site. If you need help with this part of the project, bring your drawing to a garden center to get assistance for choosing plants, or consult with a landscape designer.

Opposite: On large projects, draw your ideas in plan form before setting the stone.

Below: Plan plant and stone combinations based on the mature size of the plants.

Top right: The relationship of stones to one another is an important design element.

Bottom right: Stones at the bottom of a hill serve as a backdrop for spring flowers.

Techniques and Tools

Once you know the size (approximate dimensions and weight) and shape (natural or dressed) of the stone you want to use, it will be easier to figure out what equipment will work best to set it. The most versatile piece of equipment to set large stone is an excavator with an articulating bucket and detachable thumb. It can excavate the site, replace subsoil with gravel, set and reposition stones, and backfill the site with topsoil and mulch material after the stones are in place.

Site Preparation

Site preparation specific to setting large stone involves either digging holes to set the stones into or making level areas on which to set the stones. To make level areas, you may have to remove or add soil or gravel to create a stable spot at the right height. For long-term stability, always add fill in uniform layers.

Calculate Stone Height. If the height of individual stones is critical, try to get the height right the first time. It's especially cumbersome to raise stones, particularly if you're relying on hand tools to move them. (See "Setting Stone Height," opposite.)

Rule-Breaker Design

The design at right is a good example of how logic and site-specific traits should prevail over rules of thumb and generalizations. In this case, the recommendation to bury ⅓ of the stone would interfere with the design. Just eyond the cultivated area that includes this composition, natural boulders of a similar size sit on top of the ground, as if someone had pushed them over the steep bank that encloses, and is part of, the garden. There is also a large natural rock area that you either pass or see ahead of you as you approach this stone grouping. From either direction, the grouping ties the pre-existing site features to the cultivated ones. The composition also makes a more subtle contribution, marking the lowest elevation and the turning point at this end of the garden.

Above: Rely on the site to help guide your design choices when placing large stones.

Setting Stone Height

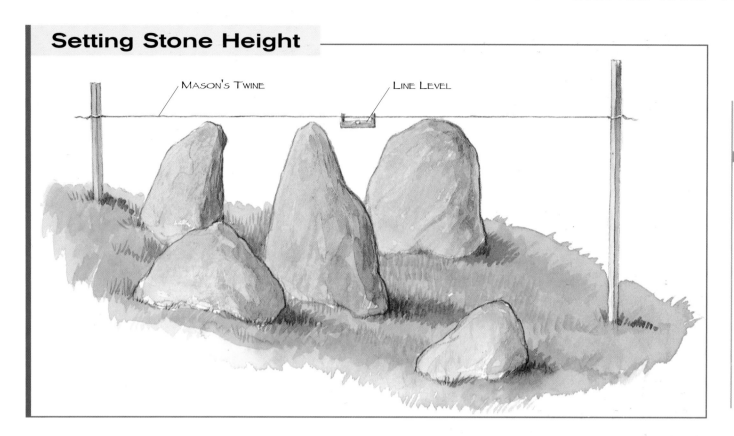

MASON'S TWINE

LINE LEVEL

Opposite: A grouping of large stones separates the street from the lawn.

Right: These large stones appear to support the level area from below.

The easiest way to get heights right in a stone composition is to use a transit and a fixed point from which to take readings. A low-tech method using string and stakes works, too. Use two or more stakes, depending on the configuration of your composition.

Judging Height. Tie a piece of mason's line taut and level between the stakes at the height of the tallest stone. Measure down from this line to set shorter stones, or use additional stakes and lines. To set a stone at a specific height, you need to know the total height of the stone, the depth of the hole, and the amount of the stone that you want exposed above ground. This isn't so difficult on a relatively level site, but if the site is sloped, you may need disproportionately taller stones to get the effect you want.

Drainage. Add drainage if your site is wet. The last thing you want is to have one or more stones in your composition list, or tip over, or to have the entire composition slowly slide down an incline.

Placing Stones with Hand Tools

The series of illustrations below shows the various ways you can move a 100- to 300-pound stone into position with hand tools, depending on the specifics of the installation, site conditions, and your ingenuity. If you use weight-rated tools like a come-a-long, you'll need to make some allowance for resistance if you pull stone along on the ground.

Keep small rocks handy to use as wedges. You'll use these to tweak the position of your stones and to hold stones in place until the backfilling is complete. Lengths of 2×4 or an iron bar are also handy for bracing stones temporarily.

Combine Techniques. In many instances, you will use a combination of techniques to get stone in place. For example, you may drag stone to the site with a chain and a truck from another location on your land. Then you may use a plank and rollers, a plank and pivot, or a come-a-long to get the stone next to the hole. To push the stone into position, you may 'walk it' into place with pry bars, slide it on a plank, or push it with the bumper of your truck or a tractor bucket. In some instances, it may be easier to push a stone into a hole if one of the sides of the hole has been excavated to make an earthen ramp.

By now you're probably getting the idea that there's no one way to work with large stone. It's true. But if you think through your options and experiment with unfamiliar tools, you'll figure out what works best for you.

Pry Bar. Pry bars are great for fine tuning stone placement. Use one or more pry bars to turn, tilt, or angle a stone into the desired position. A prybar can be used in combination with a fulcrum to increase your ability to tilt the stone. You can also use pry bars to walk a stone into position.

Stone-Setting Techniques

Pry Bar

Plank and Rollers

Come-a-long

Come-a-long. There are two common situations for using a come-a-long. Use it in combination with a chain or harness of some sort to move stones short distances by dragging them along the ground. Or use it in combination with a tripod to lift a stone and set it into position.

Plank and Rollers. This was the method of choice to move the massive blocks used to build the pyramids. You can make rollers out of metal or PVC pipe or wood. They work best on even ground.

Tripod. A tripod is a three-legged support you make on-site and use in combination with a come-a-long, winch, chain-falls, or block and tackle. With this setup you can lower the stone into position and easily turn it to get it positioned. You can also easily raise the stone to add or remove fill.

Cant Hook. A cant hook is a traditional logging tool used to roll and move logs. It also works well to move stone. With a cant hook, one person can grab, tilt, rotate, and roll a surprisingly large stone. The downside is you can't help but mar the stone if you use one. When you grab a stone, "hook" it in a place that will eventually be buried or concealed.

Ball Carts. Garden centers and landscapers use ball carts to move large plants. If this is a suitable way to move your stone, you may be able to rent one from a landscaper or garden center. Ball carts come in different sizes so match the load rating to the size of stones you want to move.

Chain or Rope. Use chain or rope to drag stones from one spot to another. Because there is a lot of resistance from the ground, use chain or rope rated for at least 2 times the estimated weight of your stone. You can move large stones with less drag, and less power, if you use a skid or plank and rollers in combination with the rope or chain.

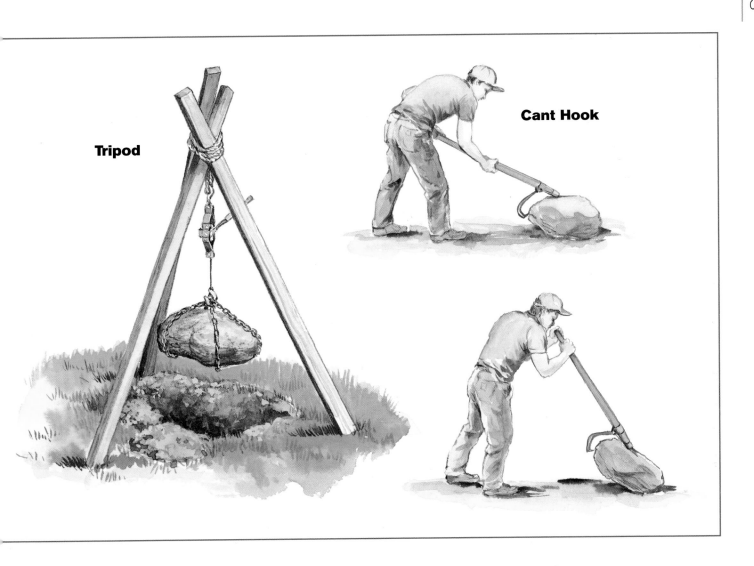

Tripod

Cant Hook

Earthmoving Equipment

To speed up the pace of the work or take it easy on your back, use an excavator, bulldozer, bobcat, or tractor to set stones that weigh more than 300 pounds. In the project shown on page 152, setting the stones that make the grade change took about 4 hours for a skilled operator and landscaper who often work together. The work proceeded quickly for this reason and because many of the stones and the fill materials were positioned within reach of the excavator bucket.

In that time they were able to install gravel fill (for drainage, stability, and proper elevation), set the stones, and distribute a 6-inch layer of topsoil over the area. Even the most skilled operator needs someone on the ground working with a shovel to either add or remove fill, position the stones, and even out the layers of fill and topsoil.

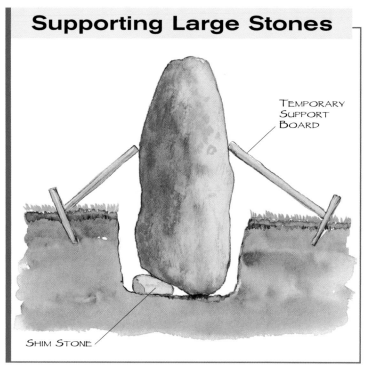

Supporting Large Stones

TEMPORARY SUPPORT BOARD

SHIM STONE

Protect the Stone

It takes forethought to minimize the chipping, gouging, and scratching of the stone during an installation. You can reduce the amount of visible damage by identifying the exposed faces of the stone beforehand and then moving the stone in a way that protects the exposed faces. If you're using an excavator or bobcat, orient the stones so that the teeth don't come in contact with the good faces when you move the stone. Furniture-moving pads or blankets are sometimes useful to protect stone. While damage is unfortunate, most damage that occurs at installation will weather and blend in over time.

Fine-Tune Your Composition. If possible, set each stone, but don't backfill for a day or two. This gives you time to discover and fix minor flaws before you finish the job. If that's not possible, try to take at least a few hours' break before final backfilling.

Above left: Native stone placed side by side forms an enclosure for a garden.

Left: Proper drainage on an incline helps provide stability for the stones you set.

Opposite: When moving stones, protect the part of the stone that will be exposed.

Working with an Equipment Operator

Before you can hire an equipment operator (or rent the equipment), you must determine exactly what it is you want to do and the general site layout. This will help the operator know which size and type of equipment is necessary to do the job. Have the following information at hand when you call a heavy-equipment operator:

- Number and size (approximate weight) of stones
- Buried services
- Water on the site
- Amount of space to maneuver equipment, or reach needed
- Topography of the site
- Site plan

- Timeline for project (During peak construction times, operators are sometimes booked months in advance. If your project is small and you can be flexible, sometimes they can work you into their schedule.)

Find an operator who has done this kind of work before and has a reputation for quality work. Garden centers and landscape designers should be able to provide you with names. Once you have selected one or two possible operators, check their references, and make an appointment for them to visit the site. Ideally, you want to hire an operator who enjoys this kind of work and is willing to work collaboratively with you. A skilled and reputable equipment operator can save you time and money.

6

SETTING LARGE STONES

Setting Specimen Stones

MULCH

2"–6" TOPSOIL

SHIM STONE

4" CRUSHED STONE

UNDISTURBED SOIL

Backfilling. Once you're satisfied with the composition, you can backfill. If you include large plants in your composition, you may want to set these as part of backfilling. The availability of equipment already on site can make moving and setting the plants easier.

Specimen Stones

Specimen stones are placed in the landscape for aesthetic reasons and are not usually part of a functional garden feature. You can use a single specimen stone or arrange them in groups of 3, 5, 7, or more. Except for instances where absolute symmetry is required, it's easier to make a visually pleasing composition with odd numbers of stones. In this picture of an enclosed garden, the single large specimen stone is black with a rough-ridged surface that is uncommon in the area. However, because the garden is completely enclosed—it's own world—a "foreign" stone does not seem out of place. Two smaller stones of the same geological type peek out from lush groundcover about 15 feet away from the large stone. Even though that distance would be too great in most compositions with stones this size, in this instance it's acceptable because the perimeter fence keeps the stones connected within the totality of the garden.

Above: Specimen stones usually have an aesthetic rather than a functional purpose.

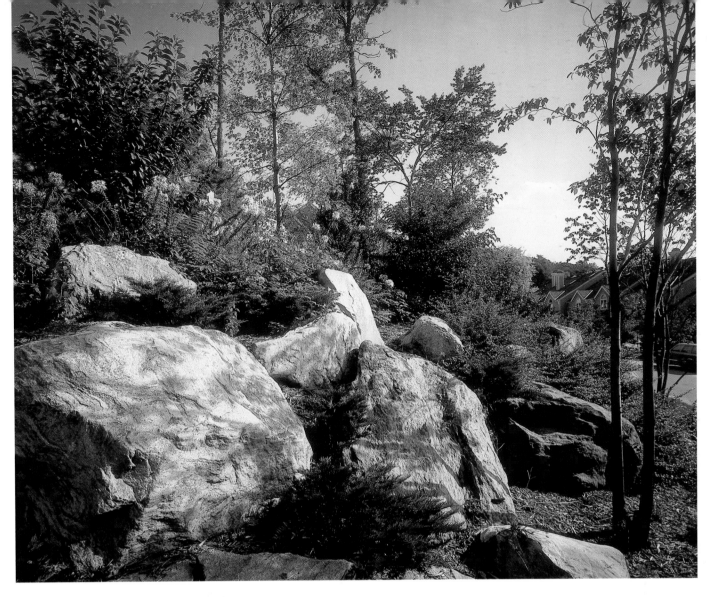

Opposite: Specimen stones will become a focal point in your design.

Above: For safety, match the equipment you use to the stone.

Matching Equipment to the Job

Here's the type of equipment you will need to move large stones. For this table, the size of stone is calculated at 160 pounds to the cubic foot. Always check with the earth-moving equipment company for capacity recommendations.

up to 300 lbs. or 2 cu. ft.	30–35 hp tractor w/bucket
up to 2,500 lbs. or 15.5 cu. ft.	60–80 hp tractor w/bucket
up to 2,000 lbs. or 12.5 cu. ft.	700 series bobcat
up to 4,000 lbs. or 25 cu. ft.	800 series bobcat
up to 10,000 lbs. or 62.5 cu. ft.	bulldozer, crane, or
	29,000-lb. excavator

Backfilling may include several layers of different materials. First use gravel or well-draining soil from the site to keep the stones stable. Leave enough room for 4 to 8 inches of topsoil, depending on your planting plans. On top of this, you may want to add several inches of bark mulch or crushed stone.

Safety. Safety is a concern on all landscape installations, but includes additional precautions when working with heavy equipment and big stone. Always maintain a safe distance from equipment. Use absolutely clear hand signals with the equipment operator. Stay in the operator's view. Restrict access to the site. Use equipment that is rated for the size stones with which you are working.

CHAPTER 10
Rock
Gardens

The popularity of xeriscapes—landscaping that uses very little water—less formal gardens, and Asian influences have stretched the definition of a 'Rock Garden' beyond its usual meaning. No longer is a rock garden strictly a mini re-creation of rugged terrain deliberately planted with tough alpine plants, sedums, and creeping phlox. Rock gardens have become sophisticated landscaping elements where natural stone plays as important a role as any of the selected plants.

Choose a Site

Even with a more elastic definition, the beauty and charm of a rock garden depends on siting, choice and arrangement of the stones, and finding the right balance of vegetation and stone. If you keep these considerations in mind, you will be less constrained when selecting plants to use in the design. (See "Plants for Rock Gardens," page 180.)

A natural rocky outcropping is nearly always the best choice for siting a rock garden, and often the outcropping is the inspiration for it. Adding other similar types of rock to create a garden can artfully expand even a small outcropping.

Effects of Climate. Traditional rock garden plants prefer sun. If you have a site that is partially or mostly shady, it will limit the variety of flowering plants that will bloom. However, there are many ferns, mosses, and woodland flowers that can be combined in a shady site for a striking rock garden. In shady sites, you need to evaluate how nearby large trees or shrubs will compete with your rock garden plants for water and nutrients. You will also want to consider whether leaves and plant litter will add an onerous maintenance chore.

Even with the most liberal interpretation, the essence of a rock garden is to mimic nature. Short of nature providing a choice site, look for a spot, preferably on a slope, where a rocky outcropping is plausible. If your space is limited, consider one or more container rock gardens or a small arrangement tucked away from formal elements, such as walkways, porches, and a clipped lawn.

Top left: A rocky outcropping is a good location for a rock garden site.

Left: Stone landscape steps appear to be a natural part of the setting in this garden.

Above: When selecting plants, consider the type of soil and the amount of sun the area receives.

Opposite: Steps in this rock garden lead to an informal seating area.

Prepare the Site

The scale of your project and the presence of a natural stone outcropping will determine how much preparation your site will need. For constructed gardens, at the very least you will excavate holes to set the stones securely and at aesthetically pleasing angles. Remove sod as you would to make a new flowerbed. If the soil is heavy or needs drainage or if the stones may heave from freezing, remove and save the topsoil; then excavate down 4 to 12 inches below where the stones will set, and add gravel for drainage.

Above: When setting stones for a rock garden, or any project, align them as they would appear in nature.

Right: If a slope is not available, consider using stone to construct planters or use them as a border for a planting area.

Container Rock Gardens

Container rock gardens offer a way to integrate a rock garden plant collection in a decidedly urban environment or in a more formal setting, such as an entryway or patio. If they are made portable, container rock gardens can be moved into a protected area in winter or out of the sun during the hottest weather.

Gardens in Walls

A rock garden wall is an alternative to a traditional rock garden. You might consider building one where there are space or topography limitations or where a wall would serve some other landscape design function.

Right: When selecting plants, take their growing patterns and size at maturity into consideration.

Below: A grouping of stone on a level area forms an island in the landscape. These plants complement the natural colors of the stone.

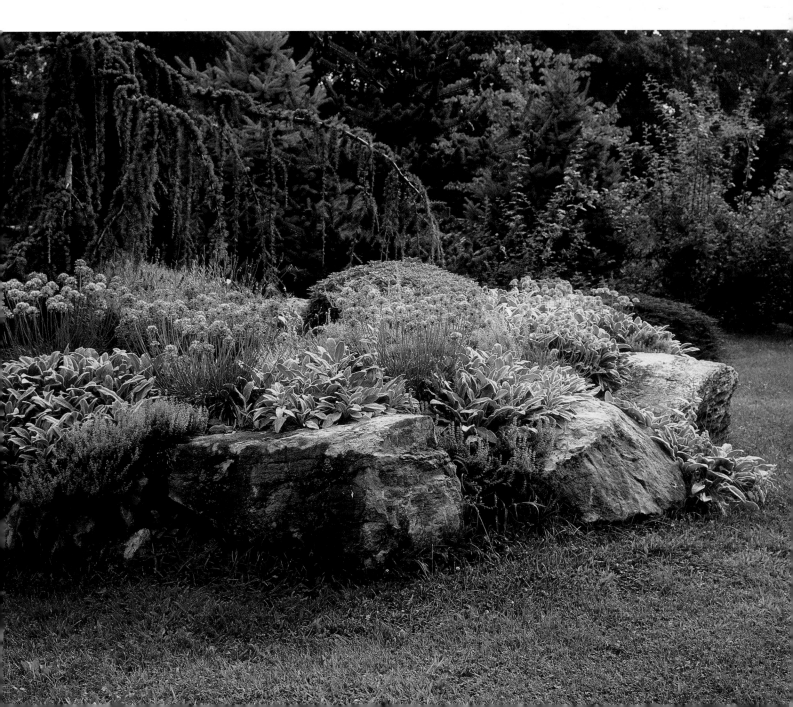

Plant as You Build. Typically, the plants are installed as the wall is built. To make the planting pockets in the wall, line the planting area with landscape fabric and partially fill the space with a soil mix suitable for the plant. Set the plant in place, and add as much additional soil as possible. Then gently tamp the soil, and water it thoroughly. You can cover the planted area with another piece of landscape fabric. If the planted area is not going to get covered with stone right away, cover the soil with wet burlap or mulch to protect the soil from drying out or being washed away.

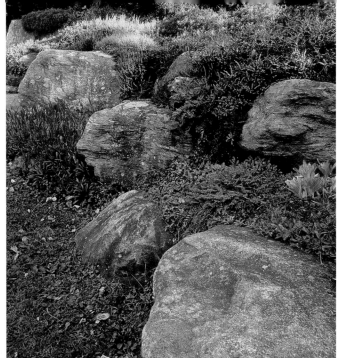

Plants in walls are more vulnerable to weather extremes. Hand watering may be needed. To limit maintenance demands, you'll want to select plants for hardiness under extremely cold or dry conditions.

Sometimes a site can accommodate a stepped wall in a way that creates larger planting pockets. This can mean less demanding maintenance and allows you to use a wider variety of plants, including small shrubs.

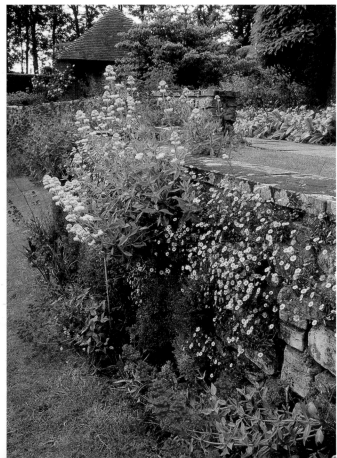

Above: For rock garden walls, choose plants that can thrive under harsher than normal conditions.

Top right: It may be necessary to amend the soil when creating a rock garden wall.

Right: If possible, choose plants that will display a variety of colors throughout the growing season.

Planting a Dry-Laid Wall

SPHAGNUM MOSS

SOIL

PLANTING

ROOT FAN

PLANTING

BACKFILL

Choose the Stone

When selecting stone for a rock garden or a garden wall, keep in mind that stone native to the area conveys belonging. On the other hand, you may want to use stone from another place to create a focal point.

Whatever your basis for choosing stone for a rock garden, its aesthetic value and structural importance are key to a successful project. The stones provide the frame, foundation, or skeleton—depending on how you look at it—of the garden. With your well thought-out planting plan in hand, arrange the stones to feature and complement your favorite plants.

Right: Clumps of brightly colored spring bulbs add a pleasing contrast to the muted tones of the natural stone.

Future Planning

If you plant your rock garden over a number of years, place pieces of plastic covered with mulch over future planting areas. This will reduce the amount of weed seed that can germinate.

Number of Plants. As with many landscaping decisions, there is no absolute ratio of stone to plants in a rock garden. One-third stone and two-thirds plants is a commonly cited ratio. In reality your site, maintenance demands, and personal preferences can easily stretch the range from as little as 20 percent to 60 percent stone.

Above: Rock gardens offer the opportunity to introduce unique textures into the landscape.

Opposite: Pond kits and liners make it easy to include a water feature in your design.

Left: Combining the right stone with the right plant can create pockets of surprise in your rock garden.

Arrange the Stone

When it comes to arranging the stones in a rock garden, there is general agreement on some basic design principles. The first: let nature be your teacher.

- Use one kind of stone. However, in large gardens you may introduce a different kind of stone as a special feature.

- If you use crushed stone mulch, try to match the color of it to the dominant stone used in the garden.

- Use sun and prevailing wind exposure to set stones in a way that creates microclimates.

- Bury at least one-half of each stone or up to the stone's widest part. You'll want the stones to look settled into the ground, not sitting on top of it.

- Arrange the stones so that grain, striations, or fracture lines are all pointed in the same direction.

- Use stones of various sizes, placing the largest at the top of the garden.

After you have arranged all the stones, study your composition for a few days or longer. If possible, set key plants where you plan to plant them. Now is the time to make changes in your composition. After the stones are set, redistribute the topsoil around the stones and make pockets of special soil mixes for specific plants.

Water in a Rock Garden

Adding moving water to a rock garden where it is not naturally present adds a level of complexity to the project. However, adding a feature that contains still water is a much easier task. Sometimes you can find a stone with a hollow spot in it, making a natural basin for a small reflecting pool. Clay pots, stone bowls, and metal cans sunk in the ground and painted black can all make satisfactory reflecting pools. You can also make shallow free-form shapes using plastic pond liner material.

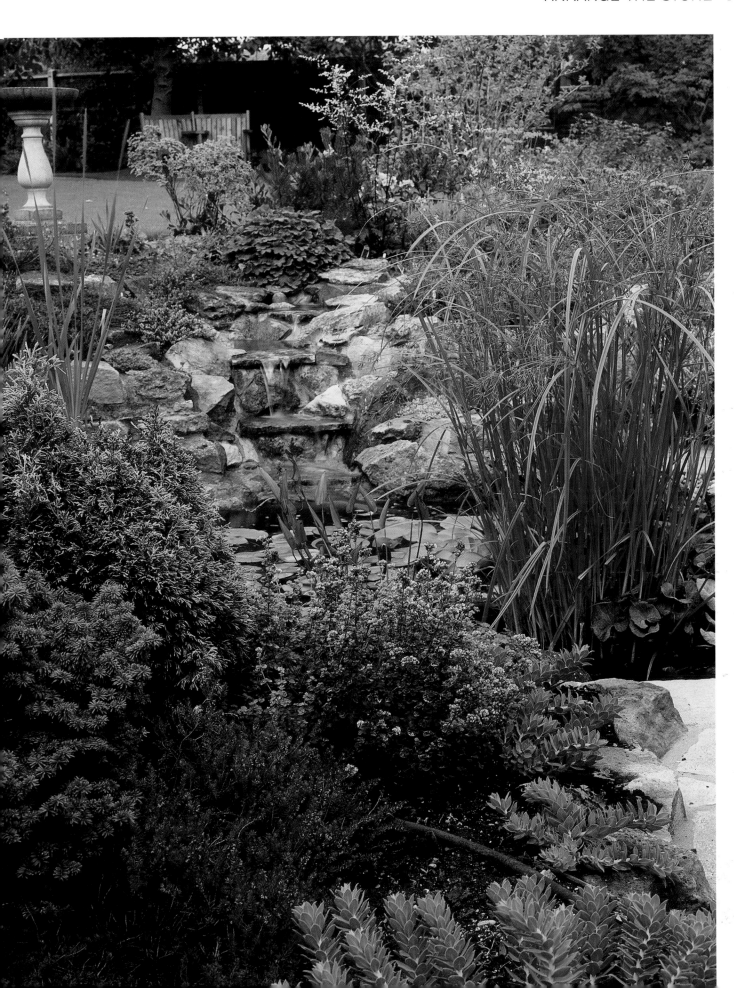

Plants for Rock Gardens

Name	Common	Zone	Ht.	Bloom	Color	Notes
Grasses						
Carex humilis	**Blue sedge**	5–9	6"–8"	Late summer	Tawny	Good ground cover in rock gardens; holds soil; forms clumps.
Festuca cinerea	**Blue fescue**	4–8	10"	Late summer	Blue foliage	Tufting; fruiting heads reach 2' tall; good with succulents.
Dwarf Conifers						
Chamaecyparis obtusa 'Nana'	**Dwarf Hinoki cypress**	4–8	1.5'	n/a	Dark green	Grows only 20" wide; leaves look like thick moss.
Juniperus communis 'Echiniformis'	**Hedgehog juniper**	2–7	2'	n/a	Clear green	The hummock-like shape adds needed contrast to a rock garden.
J. chinensis	**Sargent juniper**	4–9	2'–3'	n/a	Blue green	Adds color and shape to a rock garden.
J. squamata	**Singleseed juniper**	4–7	2'–3'	n/a	Silver green	Provides contrast for other plants.

Dwarf Hinoki cypress

Sargent juniper 'Sargentii'

Singleseed juniper 'Blue Star'

Name	Common	Zone	Ht.	Bloom	Color	Notes
Shrubs						
Calluna vulgaris	**Heather**	4–7	2.5'	Winter to spring	Range	Choose dwarf heathers; heather requires acid (6–5.5) pH soil.
Erica carnea	**Winter or spring heath**	4–7	1'	Winter to spring	White, pink, red, purple	Many cultivars are available; heath requires alkaline soil.
Rhododendron impeditum	**Yunan rhododendron**	6–8	1.5'	Spring	Purplish-blue	This dwarf shrub has tiny leaves in scale with its size.

Heather 'Corbett Red'

Scotch Heather

Scotch Heather 'Blazeaway'

Heath 'Springwood White'

Heath 'Vivelli'

Name	Common	Zone	Ht.	Bloom	Color	Notes
Perennials						
Achillea clavennae	**Silver alpine yarrow**	3–7	1'	Late spring	White	Requires alkaline (7.5) soil.
Aquilegia canadensis	**Rock columbine**	3–8	1'	Late spring	Red, yellow	Requires alkaline to neutral soil; tolerates light shade.
Aquilegia saximontana	**Colorado columbine**	4–6	4"	Spring	Blue, yellow	Requires neutral soil and a sunny location.
Arabis spp.	**Rockcress, Wallcress**	4–7	4"–1.5'	Summer	White	Requires alkaline-to-neutral soil in sunny location; many species are available.
Armeria caespitosa, A. maritima	**Thrift**	5–8	4"–8"	Early summer	Pink, white	Requires neutral soils in a sunny location; excellent cut flower, too.
Gentiana spp.	**Gentian**	3–7	2"–1.5'	Summer to fall	Blue	Several species are available; prefers sunny location.
Leontopodium alpinum	**Edelweiss**	5–7	4"–6"	Late spring-summer	Yellowish-gray/white	This traditional alpine plant requires alkaline soils in sunny locations.
Penstemon spp.	**Penstemon**	Range	Range	Spring to summer	Blue, red pink, white	Wide choice of species, cultivars; some tolerate acid soils and partial shade.
Sedum spp.	**Sedum**	Range	Range	Summer	Pink, red, yellow	Many species and cultivars are suitable.
Thymus spp.	**Thyme**	Range	Range	Late spring, summer	Pink, purple	Choose creeping species such as *T. serpyllum* & *T. pseudolanuginosus*.
Veronica prostrata	**Cliff speedwell**	5–7	6"–8"	Summer	Blue, white	Place in full sun with neutral pH soil.
Veronica spicata	**Alpine speedwell**	3–7	6"–8"	Summer	Blue, white	Place in full sun with neutral pH soil.

Armeria maritima Thrift

Penstemon 'Australis'

Penstemon 'Beard Tongue'

Penstemon 'Coccineus'

Sedum 'Autumn Joy'

Sedum

Alpine speedwell

CHAPTER 11

Freestanding
Walls

Stone walls remain popular landscape features, even if they are no longer used to confine livestock or protect gardens. A length of stone wall along the border of a garden or yard is an enduring reminder of the past, yet it is compatible with contemporary designs and lifestyles. In urban and suburban areas, you can use stone walls to establish property lines, create privacy, convey a feeling of security, define an outdoor room, or complement the rest of the landscape design.

Creating Stone Walls

There are two types of freestanding walls, dry-laid and mortared. In dry-laid stone walls, the individual stones are stacked one on top of the other without being held together with mortar, creating an informal, casual structure. This is the type of wall associated with the New England countryside, although such a wall constructed of local stone will fit anywhere.

Mortared stone walls are more formal in appearance. Bonding the stones together with mortar adds stability to the walls, but they are generally more difficult to build.

Uses for Stone Walls. With two exposed sides, a freestanding wall often does double duty in a home landscape. Viewed from the outside, a stone wall defines a boundary and adds texture to the landscape. The use of local stone helps to integrate the entire landscape design. When viewed from inside a landscape, a stone wall not only defines the boundary of a garden or the entire property but also serves as a backdrop for other landscape features.

From inside the garden, the stone wall shown on the bottom left on the opposite page is an enclosure that adds intimacy, defines a garden area, and complements the plants in the garden. Outside the garden, the wall indicates the edge of the orchard adjacent to the garden. Interestingly, the decision to build the wall was borne of an unrelated necessity—what to do with mountains of rock produced from blasting for a building foundation. The owner's decision-making process is reminiscent of an earlier time when walls were created from the stones farmers cleared from their fields.

Left: Sturdy stone walls partially enclose a small patio area.

Above: A low dry-laid wall defines the border of a large garden.

Opposite left: A traditional-looking wall marks the boundaries of a yard.

Opposite right: The wall shown here is made from native stone.

Smart Tip

Delivery Pointer

If stone is delivered on pallets, have the driver set them along the length of the wall to reduce handling on your part.

Stone for Your Wall

There are many types of stone you can use to build freestanding walls. Quarried limestone, sandstone, and slate are easy to work but not always available. Round stone or field rubble is the most difficult (some would say impossible) to use to build a stable freestanding wall, especially a dry-laid stone wall. Uniform rectilinear stone is generally more expensive and makes a more formal wall, but it is faster to lay up and an easier material with which to work.

Sorting the Stone. Unlike building a patio or walkway, you can't lay out the entire stone wall ahead of time to make aesthetic decisions about individual stones. What you can do is get to know your stone by sorting it. Set aside stones for specific purposes: the largest, flattest stones for the base course, the squarest for the ends of the wall, bond stones to span wythes, thinner flat stones for capstones, wall stones of varying sizes, and rubble to fill in between the wythes. As you sort the stone, try to visualize how you will mix the various sizes in the wall. Will you set distinctive stones in a way that contributes to a rhythm for the wall? You may want to practice laying up a section of wall to find such a rhythm.

Train Your Eye. The most important skills you need to build a sturdy and visually pleasing wall come with practice. You want to be able to select stone that fits both structurally and aesthetically in a given space, and you want to be able to make spaces to use the stones you have. Knowing your stone allows you to use both of these approaches to build your wall.

Above: Uniform, square-cut stone is easier to work with than field rubble, but it is more expensive.

Right: A garden wall such as this one is often used as a backdrop for plantings.

Opposite: Experiment with the stone you have to determine the best location for each piece.

Dry-Laid Freestanding Walls

The width of a wall depends on the wall's finished height. The base of a freestanding wall is generally one-half to two-thirds of the height. Because the stone pattern will be more random, you'll want a wider base if you're working with fieldstone rather than with semidressed or dressed stone.

Freestanding walls are usually two wythes wide, meaning that most of the stones used are only half as wide as the wall. This allows you to angle the stones toward the middle of the wall to increase the strength and durability of the wall.

Building Basics

Dry-laid walls can flex with the movement of the earth, so they do not require a concrete footing. The walls rest directly on level soil—a 6-inch-deep trench is all you need to begin building. But if the soil drains poorly or is sandy, excavate an additional 6 to 12 inches and backfill the trench to within 6 inches of the grade with compacted gravel. You get the best results if you add the gravel in 2-inch layers, compacting as you go.

An Exception to the Rule. Driveways and walkways that are cleared of snow tend to have a deeper frost line than areas that remain snow covered. If the wall abuts a plowed driveway or walkway, minimize

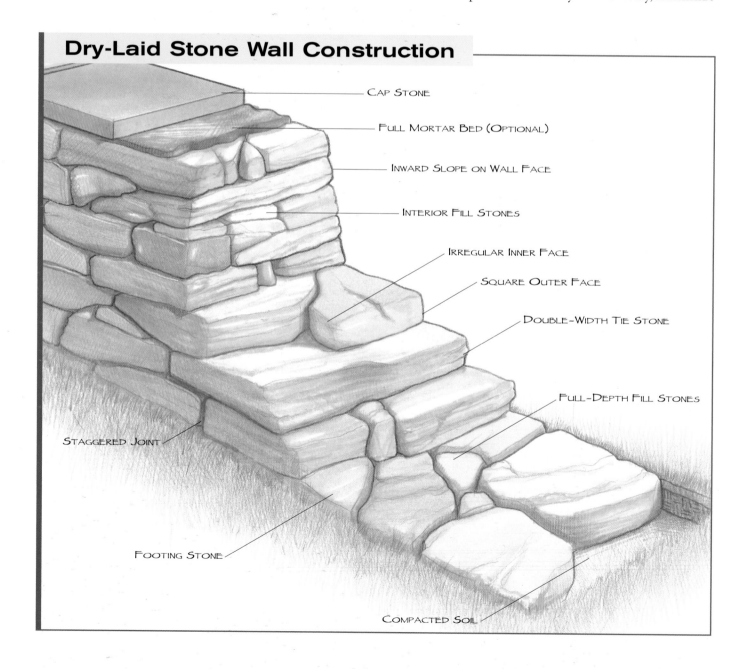

Dry-Laid Stone Wall Construction

CAP STONE

FULL MORTAR BED (OPTIONAL)

INWARD SLOPE ON WALL FACE

INTERIOR FILL STONES

IRREGULAR INNER FACE

SQUARE OUTER FACE

DOUBLE-WIDTH TIE STONE

FULL-DEPTH FILL STONES

STAGGERED JOINT

FOOTING STONE

COMPACTED SOIL

damage caused by soil heaving by installing a concrete footing below the frost line. Of course, dry-laid stone walls are easy to repair, and a small amount of damage should not be a problem. Consult local building officials as to the need for dry-laid wall footings.

Smart Tip

Picking Capstones

Select your capstones, and set them aside until you are ready to finish the top of the wall. The top is the most important face of a wall.

Left: This stone wall has obviously been in place quite a long time. Note how it has weathered the elements as compared with the wood fence.

Below: To increase stability, each side of a freestanding stone wall should tilt slightly toward the middle.

11

FREESTANDING WALLS

Types of Stone. Use the largest, flattest stones for the first course, and set them with the flattest side up. Bond stones are double-wide stones that span the entire width or both wythes of the wall; they help tie the wall together as a structure. Place bond stones at either end of the wall and every 4 to 6 feet along the length of the wall. (See "Dry-Laid Stone Wall Construction," page 188.)

As you place the stones, cant them toward the middle of the wall. This means the vertical surface of the wall will recede slightly with each course. This is called the batter. Ideally, a stone wall should have a ½- to 1-inch batter per vertical foot of height. Canting

Above: When building, install both wythes at the same time.

Left: Sort stones into categories before you start building.

Opposite: Stagger joints between the courses for strength.

Construction Tip

Stake Out the Wall

Use stakes and string to outline the base of the wall. If you will be laying stone in courses, level the lines a few inches above the height of the first course. Then measure down from the line to check your courses for level. Adjust the strings as you add more courses to the wall.

the stones in this way makes the wall more stable. You can build a wall with plumb vertical faces if you are building with dressed stone and the wall is less than 2 feet tall. (See "Make a Batter Gauge," page 204.)

It's easier to fit the stones together if you work your way down the length of the wall installing both wythes at the same time rather than installing one wythe and then going back to install the other.

After the main wall stones are set, go back and fill in between them with smaller stones. Pack the rubble between the wythes as tightly as you can without dislodging the wall stones.

The Other Courses. As you set each course on the wall, chisel or knock off projections on the stones to improve the fit and to seat the stones firmly. You can also use small wedge-shaped pieces of stone to prevent the wall stones from rocking. When you use stone wedges this way, set them deep in the wall where they are less likely to get knocked out of place.

Place stones to straddle the joints created by the stones below them: either one stone over two, or two over one. This technique, in addition to bond stones, batter, and canting the stones, contributes to the overall stability and integrity of the wall.

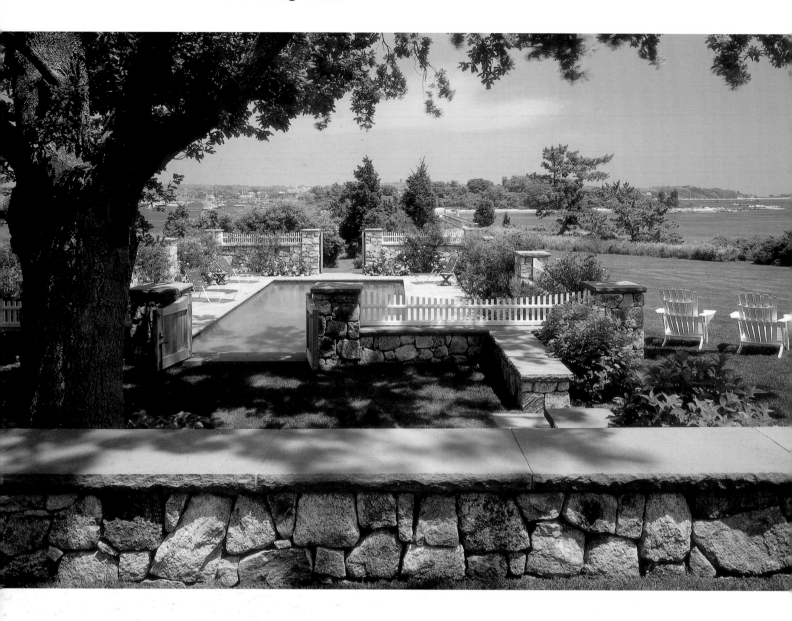

Finishing the Wall. The top courses are installed in the same way. If you have a limited number of suitable bond stones, set them in every other course. If a wall turns a corner, overlap bond stones to make the corner and connect the two walls.

As you work along, you can fill large gaps between wall stones with smaller stones. Use a hammer to tap the stones into place without displacing the wall stones.

Cap Stones. When you lay the top course, try to make it as flat and level as possible so the cap stones won't wobble.

Typically, the flattest, best-looking stones are used to cap the wall. The cap stones are generally set to overhang the rest of the wall. You can mortar the cap stones in place if they are not large and if the wall will be used as seating. Mortaring the cap stones also reduces the amount of water that gets into the wall. This protects the wall from heaving in the event of a wet fall followed by freezing temperatures before there is much snow cover.

In milder climates you can use a 2- to 4-inch-thick mortar cap. Tilt or crown the mortar cap at least $\frac{1}{8}$ inch per foot so that it sheds water.

Above: Cap stones should overhang the edges of the rest of the wall.

Opposite left: Here is an unusual cap treatment that is not used for seating.

Opposite right: These cap stones were set perpendicular to the other stones.

A Freestanding Planting Bed

With a few modifications you can make a planting bed in a freestanding wall. As a general guideline you would replace the rubble between the two wythes with high-quality soil suitable for the plants you intend to grow there. Do not reduce or eliminate the bond stones that tie the two wythes together. To hold the soil in place, install a layer of landscape fabric between the soil and the wall stones. Cut and overlap the landscape fabric to fit it around the bond stones.

Freestanding walls are one way to make gardening more accessible. A bed can be made high enough to garden from a sitting or standing position.

As with planting a retaining wall, a planting bed in a freestanding wall is a stressful environment for plants. (See "Gardens in Walls," page 175.) Plants that would survive in the ground might freeze in a freestanding planting bed. In a hot, sunny location, the maintenance watering might make planting in a freestanding wall impractical.

Mortared Freestanding Walls

A mortared stone wall gives you more flexibility for siting a wall than does a dry-laid wall. Because of the mortar between courses and a concrete footing, mortared walls can be tall yet relatively narrow.

Because mortared walls can be built narrower, they are often preferred where space is limited. You may

also want to consider mortaring a wall that will do double duty as seating or is in a living and entertainment area where a wall is apt to get leaned upon.

Mortared walls less than 4 feet tall are feasible for a homeowner with little or no experience. Like dry-laid walls, the more dressed or uniform the stone, the quicker the wall will go up. A mortared wall is more formal than a dry-laid wall and more expensive to build in cold climates.

Mortared Stone Wall Construction

CAP STONE
FULL MORTAR BED
IRREGULAR INNER FACE
SQUARE OUTER FACE
DOUBLE-WIDTH TIE STONE
CORNER STONE
STAGGERED JOINTS
EMBEDDING MORTAR
UNDISTURBED SOIL
FOOTING
COMPACTED GRAVEL
REBAR

Footing Construction

CONCRETE

REBAR

FORM BOARD

BRACE

REBAR

REBAR SUPPORT

FORM STAKE

UNDISTURBED SOIL

Concrete Footings. Because a mortared wall cannot flex with the movement of the earth, it needs a concrete footing. Typically the footing is twice the width of the wall and as deep as the wall is wide. For example, a 14-inch-thick wall would have a 28-inch-wide footing that is 14 inches thick. In cold climates, a footing must extend below the frost line to keep a wall from heaving. Once your footing is in place, building a mortared wall is similar to building a dry-laid wall.

Working with Mortar

The amount of mortar you need depends on the type of stone you use and the size of joints in the wall. A fieldstone wall will use more mortar than one built with dressed stone. To calculate how much mortar you'll need, first build a section of wall, keeping track of how much mortar you use. Multiply that amount by the number of sections of wall remaining. For example, if you build a 5-foot section and your wall is 20 feet long, you will need three times the amount you used in the first section to finish the wall. (20 divided by 5 equals 4, and one section is already complete).

If you are building with rough quarry stone or fieldstone, test-fit your stone first. Then remove the stone; make a 1- to 2-inch-thick mortar bed; and set the stone.

After one or two courses (6 to 10 inches) of wall stones are laid, pack the space between the wythes with a mixture of rubble and concrete. If you are building in courses with dressed stone, you can build up the ends of the wall after laying the first course. This helps keep the wall level, plumb, and square.

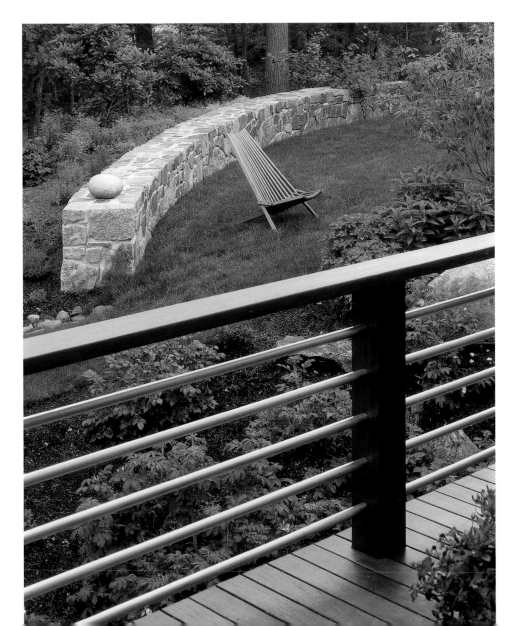

Left: A mortared wall such as this one requires a concrete footing for stability.

Setting Large Stones

If you are setting a large stone, you may need to use wedges to hold the stone in place until the mortar sets up. Scrape off excess mortar that squeezes out with the edge of your trowel.

Filling in the Spaces. After the stones in each course are set in mortar, fill the spaces between the stones. The easiest way to get mortar into the joints is to first load some mortar on your trowl; then with a quick downward motion, fling the mortar into the joint. Clean up the joints by removing excess mortar using your trowel. Follow by using a wet sponge to wipe off mortar that gets on the face of the stone. Remove this mortar as soon as possible.

Tooling the Joints. Smooth the mortar joints with a mason's jointing tool, a piece of wood with the end rounded, or a round-headed bolt sized for your joints. The tooled joints help shed water, and they contribute to the overall look of the finished wall. There are a variety of options here, so study other stonework to see which type of joint you like best. It is possible to mortar a wall built with field-stone or semidressed stone so that to the casual observer the mortar doesn't show.

Time for Tooling. When you tool the joints is more critical than how. Test the mortar by pushing your thumb into it. When the mortar is firm but you can still leave an imprint, the mortar is ready for tooling. The amount of time it takes for the mortar to get to this stage varies with temperature, humidity, and sun and wind exposure. Cover sections of wall with wet burlap to slow down the drying time. Setting a timer as a reminder to check the mortar is helpful, especially when you are still establishing a routine for laying up stone, filling joints, and tooling them.

Use a whisk broom to remove loose bits of mortar and smooth out the surface of the joints. If needed, use a wire brush to remove any mortar that may still be stuck to the stones. **Caution:** soft stone, such as sandstone, could become marred from excessive brushing. Test a piece of stone before using a wire brush on it.

Above: Tooled joints look better on a mortar wall, and they help the wall shed water.

Right: Estimate mortar needs by building a section of wall and then multiplying by the number of sections.

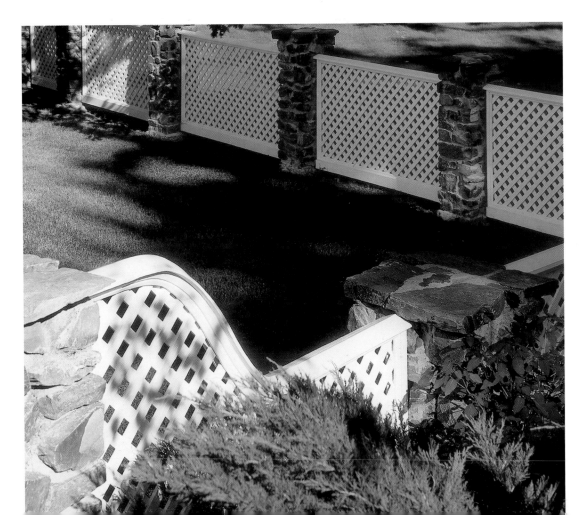

Above: For best results, try to remove mortar from the face of the stone as quickly as possible.

Left: Stone columns combine with lattice fencing to frame a yard. Columns such as these should be placed on concrete footings.

CHAPTER 12

Retaining
Walls

Retaining walls let you alter the grade or slope of the land to create level areas that you can use for planting, adding a patio, or any one of a number of uses. They also protect the slope from eroding or collapsing. As with freestanding stone walls, you can build a dry-laid wall or a mortared version. Dry-laid walls are informal and do not require a concrete footing, so they are easier to build than mortared retaining walls. Mortared walls offer more stability, but they tend to be more difficult to build.

Retaining-Wall Designs

The featured project below illustrates some of the other benefits of building stone retaining walls. By adding a wall to an uninspired level lawn, this homeowner achieved several goals. She created a sunken garden room that proves an asset to her bed-and-breakfast business, and it allows her to indulge her passion for gardening. Because stone holds heat, the growing beds in the garden room extend the harvest season and accelerate plant growth without protective covers. The heat-trapping effect of the design also extends the season for using the area as an outdoor sitting room.

The walls in the sunken garden of this ambitious project are a good example of retaining wall construction. With thoughtful, creative planning you can build a dry-laid retaining wall that is handsome, durable, and an asset to your landscape.

Right: Building with rounded stone is challenging and best used on short walls.

Below: Retaining walls create a sunken garden room that extends the normal growing season.

Opposite bottom: An evergreen shrub softens the transition between the lawn area and the wall.

Preparing the Site

Begin by calculating the height of the wall. Usually, the angle of the slope determines the height of the wall—the steeper the slope the taller the wall. There are exceptions to this rule. For example, privacy walls are usually tall no matter how steep the slope against which they are built. You may want a wall at a specific height so that you can get access to a garden bed.

Tall walls are more difficult and more costly to build. Structural and drainage issues are more critical for walls more than 3 feet tall and, if you have no prior experience, should not be attempted without professional advice or assistance. The visual mass of a tall wall can also present problems. Rather than build one tall wall, consider adding terraces and building a series of shorter walls.

Walls and Permits

Before you start digging, find out whether you need a permit to build a dry-laid stone retaining wall.

Terracing a Slope. Farmers have been terracing hillsides for thousands of years. For a homeowner, the incentive usually comes from a desire to turn an otherwise uninspiring or difficult-to-maintain hillside into accessible and attractive gardens.

The shorter walls typical of terraces require less skill to fabricate, and you can construct them in stages. Terraces are also less expensive to construct than one tall wall, and they create an inviting destination. All the steps that apply to retaining walls apply to terracing a natural hillside or constructed berm. If the slope is steep and you want wide terraces, then you will have extra fill to remove from the site.

Excavation. Once you know the location and height of the wall, you are ready to begin excavating the site. Short walls with little slope behind them may require nothing more than removing the sod and excavating down 4 to 6 inches. On sloped ground, excavation is usually a cut-and-fill process. As you cut into the slope, you use the soil to level off another area.

Plan on excavating more soil than may appear necessary. You will need space for the wall, space to work, room for gravel backfill, and space for additional backfill to minimize pressure on the wall—an important consideration for walls that front steep, tall slopes.

In many cases, you will end up with more soil than you can use on the current project. Try to find some other landscaping use for the removed soil.

The Base of the Wall. Because they can shift with the movement of the earth, dry-laid retaining

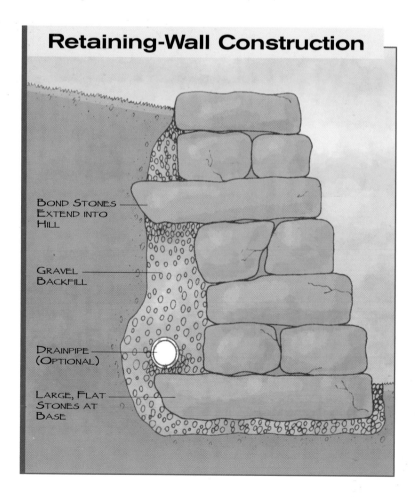

Retaining-Wall Construction

Bond Stones Extend into Hill

Gravel Backfill

Drainpipe (Optional)

Large, Flat Stones at Base

walls do not require a concrete footing. In gravelly soil that drains well, remove the sod and 4 to 6 inches of topsoil. Slope the grade in the trench ¼ to ½ inch per foot into the hill. In sandy or wet soils, excavate an additional 4 to 12 inches; lay down landscape fabric; and backfill the trench with gravel that compacts and drains.

The height of the wall will determine the width of your trench. Use this guide: for walls under 3 feet tall, make the width of the wall at its base equal to one-half the finished height of the wall; for taller walls, the width of the base should be closer to two-thirds the height of the wall. A 3-foot-tall wall should have a 2-foot-wide base. Consult a professional mason or landscape contractor when planning on a wall that is taller than 3 feet.

Mortared walls require a concrete footing. Local building codes determine the depth and width of the footing.

Left: Use retaining walls to create level areas for planting. The height of this wall makes it easy to tend to the plants shown.

Above: Rather than build one tall wall, consider building a series of shorter walls with terraces that you can then plant.

Make a Batter Gauge

Stone walls should slope inward from bottom to top. To check the inward slope as you build, construct a batter gauge from 1 x 2s joined at one end and spread apart at the other. **1** The distance between the two ends is the slope you want to maintain. To use the gauge, hold the sloping 1 x 2 against the wall, and place a level on the other board. **2** You are maintaining the right amount of batter when the level reads plumb.

Right: Retaining walls lean back into the slope. Plan on a 2-in. batter for every foot of height.

Opposite: As with freestanding walls, flat, square-cut stone is the easiest with which to work.

Drainage. Runoff from the slope will seep out between the stones of a dry-laid retaining wall. Typically, these types of walls do not require an additional drainage system. But if the site is wet and you want to minimize seepage through the wall, add a drainpipe that can move the water away from the wall. Backfilling with a few inches of coarse gravel minimizes erosion and loss of soil through the wall. For greater stability, particularly with steep slopes, lay landscape fabric between the soil and the backfill gravel.

If you are planning a mortared wall, you must provide a drainage system. Without weep holes or some other drainage system, runoff from the slope will exert tremendous pressure against the wall, resulting in buckling of the wall.

Building the Wall

When the stone is delivered to the site, sort it as you would for a freestanding wall: larger stones for the base, bond stones to span between wythes, rubble for fill between the wythes, and cap stones or coping for the top of the wall. Unlike freestanding walls, retaining walls need only one good face. If your wall is short and there isn't a lot of pressure on it, you can build the wall one stone wide provided your stones are large and good building stone, that is, they fit together well.

Calculate the Batter. Retaining walls lean back into the slope they support. This lean is called the batter. Retaining walls typically have about a 2-inch batter for every foot of height. If a wall is short and the stone is at least semidressed, you can reduce or eliminate the batter.

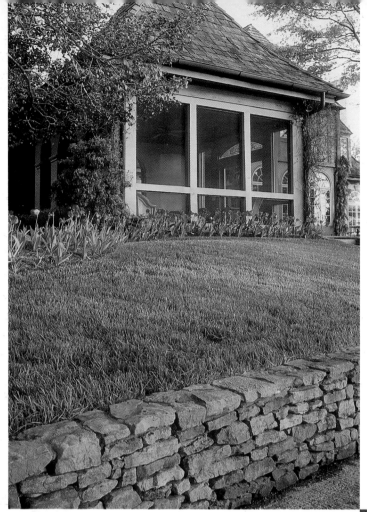

Add the Remaining Courses. Place the next course, setting it back slightly from the first. Stagger the location of the bond stones, offsetting them from the bond stones in the first course. Lay stones so that all joints between courses are staggered.

After the second course is laid, backfill with gravel and fill almost to the top of the second course. Firmly tamp the gravel in 2-inch layers. Continue laying up courses in the same manner, checking the angle of the face with your batter gauge periodically and backfilling after every two courses.

Cap the Wall. Cap stones usually span the width of the wall and protrude slightly over it. Because water can move through a dry-laid wall, the water-shedding function of the cap stones isn't as crucial. For stability, especially if the wall is located somewhere where it will be used as seating, you may want to mortar the capstones.

Lay the Base Course. Use your largest and flattest stones for the base course. Place bond stones at each end of the wall and at 4- to 6-foot intervals along the wall. Ideally, the bond stones should be long enough to extend into the slope. Between the bond stones, lay wall stones, one in front of the other, to create a double-wythe wall. Fill any gaps between these stones with smaller stones or rubble.

Tilt all the main wall stones into the hill. After laying the first course, you can backfill along the front of the wall and firmly tamp the soil in 2-inch layers. If you are going to install perforated drainpipe, now is the time to lay it along the backside of the wall. Slope the pipe to facilitate drainage.

Above: Bond stones should extend from the face of the wall into the slope that the wall supports.

Right: To facilitate drainage as you set the stones, backfill with gravel behind the wall.

Finish Backfilling and Grading. After laying the capstones, backfill with gravel up to within 4 inches or so of the top of the wall. Lay landscape fabric over the top of the gravel, and finish backfilling with soil or mulch.

Above: Mortared retaining walls require the installation of drainage pipe.

Right: Cap stones span the width of the wall and over-hang its edges slightly.

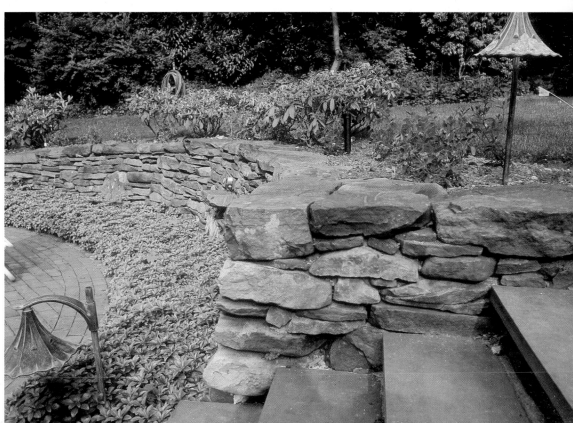

Adding a Fire Pit

Using the same techniques for building a dry-laid retaining wall, you can build a stone fire pit in an outdoor living area to add a welcoming gathering spot to your landscape. A fire pit reduces the effects of wind on a fire, and for serious stargazers it has the added benefit of containing the fire glow.

Locating the Fire Pit. Likely locations for a fire pit include in the backyard; adjacent to a patio; on a beach; or by a pond or pool. You can build a fire pit on a hillside, but you will have to level an area first. Ultimately, the absence of fire hazards will determine potential locations for a fire pit. Choose a site that is a safe distance from buildings, fuel storage, and supply lines, and from overhanging tree branches and utility wires. Beyond this, and the general site considerations in Chapter Two, build your fire pit with leisure and entertaining in mind.

Size the Fire Pit. There are no hard-and-fast rules for fire-pit proportions. A tapered pit is more engaging visually, especially if the pit is less than 5 feet in diameter. Whatever the size, you need a hole 24 to 36 inches wider than the desired finished inside dimensions. For a 36- to 42-inch-wide by 20- to 24-inch-deep pit like the ones pictured, excavate a 6-foot-diameter hole.

The depth of the hole depends on the thickness of the bottom stone(s), the type of soil, and the desired finished depth of the pit. To calculate hole depth, add up the finished depth of the pit, the thickness of the bottom stone, and the thickness of the gravel base.

Excavate the Hole. Outline the perimeter of the fire pit with a garden hose or string. If you have to remove sod, use a digging spade to cut it up. Cut through the sod around the perimeter of the hole; then cut the sod into manageable pieces. Use it to patch bare spots elsewhere, or compost it. Excavate the topsoil separately, and save it for grading afterwards.

After you excavate the hole, level the bottom. Check for level using a 4-foot carpenter's level, a straight 4-foot board, or a 2×4 on edge with a 2-foot level on top. Tamp the bottom of the hole firmly; then add at least 2 inches of gravel that compacts but also drains. In heavy soils or where there is seasonal standing water or below freezing temperatures, use up to 8 inches of gravel and tamp it in 2-inch layers.

Build the Fire Pit

To build a fire pit, you will set dry-laid stone in a cone shape. To build in the round, try to use stones with one side longer than the other. If you don't spend a lot of time shaping the stones, the wall will look good from above but can have wedge-shaped gaps between some of the stones. Fill these spaces with small nonload-bearing stones. In other words, as you build, keep the load on the wall stones as in traditional stone-wall construction.

Lay the First Course. To begin, set the stone or stones that form the bottom of the pit in the middle of the hole. Then set the first course of stones around the bottom stone. It's okay if there are gaps between the bottom and wall stones.

Calculate the Setback. To build a tapered pit, you need to calculate the setback for each course. To do this, first estimate the number of courses it will take to build the pit. To calculate the setback for each course, take ½ of the difference between the bottom and top finished diameters of the pit and divide by the number of courses. For example, for a pit 24 inches wide at the bottom and 36 inches wide at the top, the difference is 12 (36 minus 24). One-half of the difference between those two measurements is 6. If there are eight courses, divide 6 by 8, which gives you 0.75 or ¾ of an inch. In this example, each course is set back ¾ inch from the one below it.

Left: A fire pit will become a destination in your landscape design.

Fire Pit Construction

UNDISTURBED SOIL

20"–24"

2"–6" GRAVEL

Above: Flat stones form a transition from the edge of the pit to the surrounding lawn.

Add Backfill. Begin backfilling after you lay up about 6 inches of wall. Compact the backfill using a hoe, tamper, or your feet. Water the area. Repeat this process after building each successive 6 inches of wall. Some backfill will work its way through the wall over time. In other walls, landscape fabric is used to keep backfill from migrating into the stonework. In this application, the heat from the fire could eventually melt the fabric or char natural fiber burlap. You could use metal screen in place of weed-barrier fabric. Or use small rocks or crushed stone for a few inches behind the wall stones; then fill in the remaining space with some of the excavated soil. If the excavated soil is heavy clay, backfill with gravel.

Cap the Pit. When the construction is within two courses of the surrounding grade, take some rough measurements so that the fire pit surround stones end up at the level you want and can be set on a 1-inch-per-foot slope away from the pit. After you set each of the stones that edge the pit, do a safety check. Ask someone who weighs at least 150 pounds to stand on the stone and lean out over the pit as far as possible without falling in. Repeat this for each stone that edges the pit. If a stone tips up even the slightest bit, reset it or replace it. Once the construction is complete, you may have to cut or fill to make a transition from the excavation area to the surrounding grade. The photos on pages 208 and 209 show different transitions from the pit to the surroundings.

Add Seating. Permanent stone, wood, or metal bench seats are a practical amenity that turns a fire pit into an inviting destination, even without the attraction of a fire. Seating also acts as a visual clue to identify the spot from a distance.

Right: Walls made of native stone tend to blend easily with the surrounding area.

Opposite top: To increase stability, stagger the joints of the wall from one course to the next.

Opposite bottom: A retaining wall provides a planting area for brightly colored shrubs.

Resource Guide

The following list of manufacturers and associations is meant to be a general guide to additional industry and product-related sources. It is not intended as a listing of products and manufacturers represented by the photographs in this book.

American Nursery and Landscape Association (ANLA) offers educational seminars and other services to its members. The Web site offers a way to locate garden centers and landscape designers.
1000 Vermont Ave., NW
Ste. 300
Washington, DC 20015-4914
Phone: 202-789-2900
www.anla.org

Artistic Gardener offers a number of garden art molds for stepping-stones and benches. Its molds are fully reusable.
3275 NW Ivy Lane
Camas, WA 98607
Phone: 360-834-7021
www.historystones.com

Beuchel Stone Corp. provides natural, quarried stone from select cities in the United States. Its product line includes patio stone, accent boulders, and custom-cut stones for steps.
W3639 Hwy. H
Chilton, WI 53014
800-236-4473
www.buechelstone.com

Cast Stone Institute is a non-profit trade organization that aims to improve the quality of cast stone.
10 West Kimball St.
Winder, Georgia 30680-2535
Phone: 770-868-5909
Fax: 770-868-5910
www.caststone.org

The Colonial Stoneyard specializes in natural stone and stone products for landscaping projects. The company claims that it has the right stone to match anyone's style or budget.
66 North St.
Groton, MA 01450
Phone: 978-448-3329
www.colonialstoneyard.com

Concrete Foundations Association provides educational materials to contractors in 26 states and Canada.
107 First St. West
P.O. Box 204
Mount Vernon, IA 52314
Phone: 319-895-6940
www.cfawalls.org

Cooley Stone offers landscaping options with stone from quarries in northeastern Pennsylvania. The company's Web site offers a complete catalog.
RR 2, Box 154
Kingsley, PA 18826
Phone: 570-278-2355
www.cooleystone.com

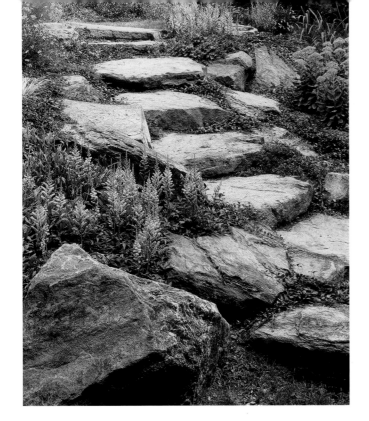

The Hearth, Patio, and Barbecue Association (HPBA) promotes the hearth products industry.
1601 N. Kent St., Ste. 1001
Arlington, VA 22209
Phone: 703-522-0086
Fax: 703-522-0548
www.hpba.org

High Plains Stone provides builders with a selection of building, masonry, and landscape stone from across America. The company's Web site includes a how-to section.
P.O. Box 100
Castle Rock, CO 80104
Phone: 303-791-1862
www.highplainsstone.com

Hi-Tech Architectural Products' Granite Paving division offers a selection of granite and concrete pavers for projects in stone. The company's Web site offers a catalog and free estimates on orders.
2950 Jefferson St., Ste. A
Riverside, CA 92504
Phone: 909-785-7592
www.granitepaving.com

The International Masonry Institute provides marketing promotional materials for the masonry industry.

The James Brice House
42 East St.
Annapolis, MD 21401
Phone: 410-280-1305
Fax: 301-261-2855
www.imiweb.org

Lang Stone Company sells home and landscaping stone to professionals and homeowners. The company's Web site features an extensive product gallery.
707 Short St.
Columbus, OH 43215
Phone: 800-589-5264
www.langstone.com

Learning Stone offers a number of links to various stone resources. Its Web site also features a stone message board where visitors can read and write posts on the subject of stonework.
www.learningstone.net

Lemke Stone, Inc., specializes in cobblestone, boulders, Lannon stone, and Bedford stone. The company supplies DIY homeowners as well as professional landscapers, masons, and contractors.
19594 W. Good Hope Rd.
Lannon, WI 53046
Phone: 262-502-1579
www.lemkestone.com

Little Meadows Stone Company offers a variety of natural stone for any landscaping project. The company's Web site offers a photo gallery of its product offerings.
RR 1, Box 1553
Little Meadows, PA 18830
Phone: 570-623-2703
www.littlemeadowsstone.com

Loukonen Brothers Stone produces Colorado red and buff sandstone for builders and landscapers. The Web site features the company's products along with its prices.
12993 N. Foothills Hwy.
Longmont, CO 80503
Phone: 303-823-6268
www.loukonenbros.com

Luck Stone Corporation manufactures a number of construction aggregates and architectural stone. The company's Web site features a product listing and location guide.
P.O. Box 29682
Richmond, VA 23242
Phone: 800-898-5825
www.luckstone.com

Marshalltown Trowel Company sells a variety of quality tools to homeowners and masonry professionals.
104 South 8th Ave.
Marshalltown, IA 50158
Phone: 641-753-5999
Fax: 641-753-6341
www.marshalltown.com

The Mason Contractors Association of America (MCAA) represents mason contractors' needs and promotes the use of masonry through a variety of programs. The organization sells technical manuals dealing with all types of masonry work.
33 S. Roselle Rd.
Schaumberg, IL 60193
Phone: 800-536-2225
www.masoncontractors.org

The Masonry Advisory Council provides the public with general and technical information about masonry design and detail. Its Web site contains articles and a guide to brick selection.
1480 Renaissance Dr.
Ste. 302
Park Ridge, IL 60068
847-297-6704
www.maconline.org

The Masonry Society is an international group interested in the science, art, and advancement of masonry.
3970 Broadway, Ste. 201-D
Boulder, CO 80304-1135
Phone: 303-939-9700
Fax: 303-541-9215
www.masonrysociety.org

National Stone, Sand, and Gravel Association (NSSGA) represents the aggregate industries. Its member companies produce more than 90 percent of the crushed stone used annually in the United States. Visit the association's Web site for workshop and conference information.
1605 King St.
Alexandria, VA 22314
703-525-8788
www.nssga.org

Natural-stone.com is a Web resource that focuses mostly on the consumer and business-to-business side of the natural stone industry. The Web site has a company locator and a stone search guide.
www.natural-stone.com

Northeast Stone Works is the producer of an extensive natural stone line, including boulders, wall stone, and slabs for steps. Visit the company's Web site for more information about its products.
RR 1, Box 1 BB
Springville, PA 18844
Phone: 570-278-8768
www.northeaststone.com

Rolling Rock Building Stone, Inc., offers its own building products, as well as stone varieties from Asia, Brazil, Canada, and Mexico. Visit the photo gallery at the company's Web site.
40 Rolling Rock Rd.
Boyertown, PA 19512
Phone: 610-987-6226
www.rollrock.com

Select Stone, Inc., offers natural stone from the United States, as well as Europe and Asia. The company provides stone to residential and commercial construction projects throughout the U.S.

P.O. Box 6403
Bozeman, MT 59771
Phone: 888-237-1000
www.selectstone.com

The Stone Foundation is a society of stonemasons and others involved with and interested in stone and stone-work. Visit its Web site for more information about workshops and symposiums.
116 Lovato Lane
Santa Fe, NM 87505
Phone: 505-989-4644
www.stonefoundation.org

Stone Info.com, a division of KD Resources, has a Web site that offers valuable information to construction professionals.
8711 E. Pinnacle Peak Rd.
Scottsdale, AZ 85255
Phone: 480-502-5354
Fax: 781-394-0599
www.stoneinfo.com

Stone Wholesale Corporation supplies landscape stone, moss rock boulders, and decorative building stone from its own quarry. View the company's Web site for pictures and price lists.
4717 West Lakeview Dr.
Ft. Collins, CO 80526
Phone: 877-221-0057
www.stonewholesalecorp.com

Stone World magazine offers information on stone architecture as well as stone production, distribution, installation, and maintenance. Its Web site offers industry news and a buyer's guide.
BNP Media
210 Route 4 East, Ste. 311
Paramus, NJ 07652
Phone: 201-291-9002
www.stoneworld.com

Stone-X is a directory that promotes the use of natural stone for the construction industry. Stone-X aims at improving business by sharing expertise, knowledge, and experience. Stone-X can be contacted through its Web site.
www.stone-x.com

Metric Equivalents

All measurements in this book are given in U.S. Customary units. If you wish to find metric equivalents, use the following table and conversion factors.

Length

1 inch	25.4 mm
1 foot	0.3048 m
1 yard	0.9144 m
1 mile	1.61 km

Area

1 square inch	645 mm^2
1 square foot	0.0929 m^2
1 square yard	0.8361 m^2
1 acre	4046.86 m^2
1 square mile	2.59 km^2

Volume

1 cubic inch	16.3870 cm^3
1 cubic foot	0.03 m^3
1 cubic yard	0.77 m^3

Capacity

1 fluid ounce	29.57 ml
1 pint	473.18 ml
1 quart	1.14 l
1 gallon	3.79 l

Weight

1 ounce	28.35g
1 pound	0.45kg

Temperature

Fahrenheit = Celsius × 1.8 + 32
Celsius = Fahrenheit - 32 × ⅝

Nail Size & Length

Penny Size	Nail Length
2d	1"
3d	1¼"
4d	1½"
5d	1¾"
6d	2"
7d	2¼"
8d	2½"
9d	2¾"
10d	3"
12d	3¼"
16d	3½"

Glossary

Aggregate Crushed stone, gravel, or other material added to cement to make concrete or mortar. Gravel and crushed stone are considered coarse aggregate; sand is considered fine aggregate.

Ashlar Any stone cut to a square or rectangular shape in either random or uniform sizes. Also, a pattern for laying courses of rectangular blocks of stone.

Backfill Sand, gravel, pea stone, or crushed stone used to refill excavated areas with a stable, porous material.

Batter The angle or slope of a stone wall from base to top that is necessary for stability.

Bed Horizontal masonry joint, sometimes called bed joint. Also, any prepared surface (stone, gravel, sand, or mortar) for placing stone.

Belgian blocks Stone cut in square or rectangular shapes, usually about the size of a large brick, and used for paving.

Bondstone A long stone used to tie the wythes together in a freestanding wall. Sometimes called a through stone.

Building surface The faces or surfaces of a stone that carry and distribute the load in a wall, typically the surfaces that are the top and bottom of a wall stone.

Capstones Stone used to form the top course of a wall.

Chinkers Small, irregularly shaped stones used to fill gaps in a wall.

Cobblestone Any small-dimension milled stone that is used for paving.

Concrete A mixture of portland cement, sand, gravel or crushed rock, and water that forms a solid material when cured.

Coping The top layer of stones on a wall, usually slightly wider than the wall, sometimes called cap-stones. Also, the individual stones that make up the finished edge around a pond or pool.

Courses The horizontal layers of stones in a wall. Also, the rows of uniform-sized stone or pavers used to make a walk or patio.

Crazy paving Irregularly shaped pieces of stone used to make a walk or patio.

Crushed rock Small-dimension material available in a range of colors and sizes with rough, angular surfaces.

Curing The process by which concrete becomes solid and develops strength.

Cut stone Any stone that has been milled or worked by hand to a specific shape or dimensions.

Dressed stone Usually quarried stone that has been squared-off on all sides and has a smooth face.

Dry wall A stone wall constructed without mortar.

Excavation To remove earth or soil so that the construction will be supported by a subgrade that is hard, uniformly graded, and well drained.

Face The exposed side of a stone.

Fieldstone Stone as it is found in the natural environment.

Flagging Paving for walks or patios made from flagstone.

Flagstone Any stone milled to a uniform thickness of 1 to 2 inches to use for walk and patio surfaces. Flagstone is available in uniform rectangular shapes or in random shaped pieces sometimes called crazy paving.

Footing Support for mortared stonework generally made of concrete and extending below the frost line to avoid problems from frost heaves.

Frost heave Shifting or upheaval of the ground resulting from alternate freezing and thawing of water in the soil.

Frost line The maximum depth to which soil freezes in the winter. Frost line depth varies from region to region and is deeper under areas that are cleared of snow in winter, such as walkways, steps, and driveways.

Ground-fault circuit interrupter (GFCI) A safety circuit breaker that compares the amount of current entering a receptacle with the amount leaving it. If there is a discrepancy, the GFCI breaks the circuit and stops the current. The device is required by electrical code in areas that are subject to dampness.

Hardscape That portion of a landscape that is made of nonliving material, such as concrete, stone, or lumber.

Mason's line A kind of twine used by masons that can be stretched taut. It is used to lay out projects, check for level, and as a straightedge guide to check the evenness of a course as it is being laid.

Microclimate An area in a landscape with growing conditions that differ from the rest of the landscape. The differences can be caused by variances in the amount of sunlight received, wind currents, topography, and other factors.

Mortar A mixture of cementitious materials, fine aggregate, and water. Mortar is used to bond bricks or blocks.

Nominal dimensions The dimensions of a masonry unit plus one mortar joint.

Pea gravel Small rounded stone most often used in gravel gardens or for walkways.

Portland cement A mixture of burned lime, iron, silica, and alumina. This mixture is put through a kiln, ground into a fine powder, and packaged for sale.

Prepackaged concrete mix A mix that combines cement, sand, and gravel in the correct proportions and requires only the addition of water to create fresh concrete.

Ready-mix concrete Wet concrete that is transported from a concrete supplier. The concrete is ready to pour.

Rebar Reinforcing bar that is used for concrete that will carry a heavy load, such as footings, foundation walls, columns, and pilasters.

Retaining walls A wall built to hold back sloping ground or make a grade change. Retaining walls can be dry-laid or mortared.

Pavers Any stone milled to a uniform size and shape, typically about the size of a brick, and used to surface walkways and patios.

Quarry dressed Stone that is squared-off on all sides but has a rough face. Sometimes called semidressed stone.

Riverstones Small- to medium-sized stones that are worn or rounded from water.

Rough stone Stone as it comes from the quarry.

Screeding Moving a straight board, such as a 2×4, back and forth across the tops of forms to smooth and level sand or concrete.

Stand-alone fountain A fountain that has its own reservoir and does not require a pond. (Also called a self-contained fountain.)

Steel reinforcement Reinforcing mesh or rebar that is used to strengthen concrete.

Tamp Compacting gravel or sand in 2- to 4-inch layers to form a solid base for flat stonework, such as a patio.

Tamper A hand tool or power device used to compact soil or gravel so that it is less likely to shift or crumble.

Through stone A long stone used to tie the wythes together in a freestanding wall. Sometimes called a bondstone.

Topsoil The uppermost layer of soil; it is the most fertile and workable for gardeners.

Weep hole A hole in a mortared retaining wall that allows water to seep through to relieve pressure against the wall. Typically formed by embedding a length of plastic or metal pipe in a mortar joint.

Wythe The vertical section of a wall that is one stone or one masonry unit wide.

GLOSSARY

Index

Credits

R: Right, L: Left, T: Top, B: Bottom, C: Center

page 1: Charles Mann page 2: Alan and Linda Detrick page 6: Brian Vanden Brink Photos/Todd Caverly page 7: (T) Brian Vanden Brink; (B) Walter Chandoha page 8: (T) Positive Images/Ben Phillips; (B) Charles Mann page 9: Walter Chandoha page 10: Alan and Linda Detrick page 11: *both* Tony Giammarino pages 12–13: Tony Giammarino page 14: Alan and Linda Detrick page 15: (T) Michael Thompson; (B) Walter Chandoha page 16: (T) Jerry Pavia; (B) Alan and Linda Detrick page 17: (T) John Glover; (C) Walter Chandoha; (B) Jessie Walker page 18: (T) Ken Druse; (B) Alan and Linda Detrick page 19: John Glover page 20: Brian Vanden Brink Photos/Todd Caverly page 21: (TL), (TR) Alan and Linda Detrick; (BR) Michael Thompson; (BL) Alan and Linda Detrick page 22: (T), (C) Walter Chandoha; (BL) Jerry Pavia page 23: (T) Brian Vanden Brink; (B) John Glover page 24: (TR) Jerry Pavia; (BR) Brian Vanden Brink, architect: Elliot, Elliot, Norelius; (LC) Alan and Linda Detrick page 25: (TL), (BR) Derek Fell; (BL) Garden Picture Library/Ron Sutherland page 26: (TL) Michael Thompson; (TR, BL) Alan and Linda Detrick; (BR) Michael Thompson, designer: Artistic Landscapes page 27: Tria Giovan page 28: (TR) Jerry Pavia; (B) Brad Simmons; (L) Jerry Pavia; (C) John Glover page 29: (TL) John Glover; (TR) Tria Giovan; (BR) Alan and Linda Detrick; (BL) Tony Giammarino, designer: Martha Stobbs Designs page 30: (TL) John Glover; (R) Brian Vanden Brink, designer: Horiuchi & Solien Landscape page 31: (TL), (TR) John Glover; (B) Brian Vanden Brink page 32: (LC) Brian Vanden Brink, architect: John Morris; (TR) John Glover; (BR) Brian Vanden Brink Photos/Todd Caverly; (BL) Brad Simmons page 33: Brian Vanden Brink, architect: Sally Weston page 34: (L) Brian Vanden Brink, architect: Mark Hutker & Associates; (TR) Walter Chandoha; (BR) Alan and Linda Detrick page 35: (T) Alan and Linda Detrick; (RC) Walter Chandoha; (BR), (BL) Jerry Pavia page 36: (TL) Jerry Pavia; (TR) Tony Giammarino, design: Maymont Gardens (BR) Jerry Pavia; (BL) Brian Vanden Brink page 37: Garden Picture Library/Marie O'Hara page 38: (L) Brian Vanden Brink; (TR) Jerry Pavia; (BR) Michael Thompson, design: Marietia and Ernie O'Byrne page 39: (TL) Garden Picture Library/John Beedle; (RC), (B) John Glover page 40: (TL) Jerry Pavia; (TR) Garden Picture Library/John Glover; (B) Garden Picture Library/Steven Wooster page 41: (T) Charles Mann; (BR) John Glover; (BL) Jerry Pavia pages 42–43: Brian Vanden Brink page 44: Michael S. Thompson page 45: Michael S. Thompson page 46: (T) Brad Simmons; (B) Charles Mann page 47: Tony Giammarino page 48: Brad Simmons page 49: Walter Chandoha page 50: Jessie Walker page 51: Brian Vanden Brink page 52: Tony Giammarino page 53: (T) Randall Perry; (B) Jerry Pavia page 54: (L) John Glover; (R) Tony Giammarino page 55: Brian Vanden Brink pages 56–57: Bill Rothschild page 58: Brian Vanden Brink page 59: John Parsekian/CH page 60: (L) Tria Giovan; (R) Brian Vanden Brink page 61: (T) Brian Vanden Brink; (B) Walter Chandoha pages 62–63: (L) John Glover; (C) Charles Mann; (TR) Garden Picture Library/John Glover; (BR) Walter Chandoha page 64: (L) Brian Vanden Brink; (R) Walter Chandoha page 65: (TR) Derek Fell; (BL) Brian Vanden Brink; (BR) Walter Chandoha page 66: Garden Picture Library/Jacqui Hurst page 67: Tria Giovan pages 68–69: Brian Vanden Brink page 70: (T) Karen Bus-

solini; (B) Charles Mann page 71: (TL), (LC), (BL), John Parsekian/CH; (BR) Brian C. Nieves/CH page 72: Garden Picture Library/Juliette Wade page 73: (T) Jerry Howard; (B) Charles Mann page 75: Charles Mann page 76: (T) Brad Simmons; (BL), (BR) John Parsekian/CH page 77: Garden Picture Library/Ron Sutherland page 78: (T) Patricia J. Bruno; (B) Charles Mann page 79: Juliet Green pages 80–81: Brian Vanden Brink page 82: (L) Brad Simmons; (R) Charles Mann page 83: Ron Evans page 84: (T) Patricia J. Bruno; (B) Tony Giammarino page 85: (T) Michael S. Thompson; (B) John Glover pages 86–87: Jessie Walker page 88: (T) Carolyn Bates, design and installation: Paul Wieczoreck, Champlain Valley Landscaping; (B) Alan and Linda Detrick page 89: Brian Vanden Brink page 91: Jerry Pavia page 92: Tony Giammarino page 93: Jerry Pavia page 94: Brian Vanden Brink page 97: (T) Garden Picture Library/Ron Sutherland; (B) Carolyn Bates, design and installation: Terry Krinsky, Distinctive Landscaping page 98: (T) Walter Chandoha, (B) Merle Henkenius page 99: Michael S. Thompson page 100–101: Jessie Walker page 102: (T), (C) John Parsekian/CH; (B) Jessie Walker page 103: Jessie Walker page 104: Jerry Pavia page 105: Garden Picture Library/Ron Sutherland pages 106–107: Bill Rothschild page 109: *both* Carolyn Bates, design and installation: Michael Lawrence Associates, Distinctive Landscaping page 110: (T) John Glover; (B) Brian Vanden Brink page 111: (C) John Parsekian/CH; (B) Ann Reilly page 112: (T) John Parsekian/CH; (B) Brian Vanden Brink page 113: (T) Karen Bussolini; (B) Alan and Linda Detrick page 115: (T) Lee Anne White; (B) Garden Picture Library/Ron Sutherland page 116: (T) John Parsekian/CH; (B) Jessie Walker page 117: (T) Carolyn Bates, design and installation: Cushman Design Group, Inc., Slayton Lanscape Construction (B) Michael S. Thompson page 118: Brian Vanden Brink page 119: Garden Picture Library/Marie O'Hara; (B) Garden Picture Library/Ron Sutherland page 120: (BL) Carolyn Bates, design and installation: Catherine Clemens, Clemens and Associates; (TR) Brian Vanden Brink page 121: (T) John Glover; (B) Tony Giammarino page 123: Garden Picture Library/Jacqui Hurst pages 124–125: (BL) John Glover; (C) Bill Rothschild; (BC) Brad Simmons; (R) Ivy Moriber pages 126–127: Brian Vanden Brink pages 128–129: (TC) Karen Bussolini; (TR) Carolyn Bates, design and installation: Landshapes; (BR) Jerry Pavia page 130: (B) Michael S. Thompson; (T) Karen Bussolini page 131: (TR) Gay Bumgarner; (B) Lee Anne White page 132: (T) Carolyn Bates, design and installation: Paul Wieczoreck, Champlain Valley Landscaping; (B) Charles Mann page 133: (T), (BR) Charles Mann; (BL) Alan and Linda Detrick page 134: Charles Mann page 135: Karen Bussolini page 136: (TR) Jerry Pavia; (B) Carolyn Bates, design and installation: Michael Lawrence Associates, Distinctive Landscaping page 137: (L), (TR) Alan and Linda Detrick; (BR) Jerry Howard pages 138–139: Michael S. Thompson page 140: (TL) Jessie Walker; (BR) Carolyn Bates, design and installation: Justin Rose, Creations in Stone page 141: (BL) John Glover; (TR) Carolyn Bates, design: Justin Rose, Creations in Stone pages 142–143: *all* Carolyn Bates page 144: *both* John Glover page 145: Jessie Walker pages 146–147: (L) John Glover; (C) Garden Picture Library/Ron Sutherland; (R) Carolyn Bates, design and installation: Catherine Clemens, Clemens and Associates pages 148–149: (L) Carolyn Bates, design

and installation: Michael Lawrence Associates, Custom Stonework; (C) John Glover; (R) Walter Chandoha pages 150–151: Brian Vanden Brink pages 152–153: (TC) Carolyn Bates, design and installation: Andrea Morgante Landscaping; (BR) Charles Mann; (BL) Jerry Pavia page 154: John Glover page 155: Tony Giammarino page 156: (LC) Charles Mann; (TR) Jerry Pavia; (BR) Jessie Walker page 157: (T) Charles Mann; (B) Jerry Pavia page 158: (L) Jerry Pavia; (R) Carolyn Bates, design and installation: Catherine Clemens, Clemens and Associates page 159: Carolyn Bates, design and installation: Pete McGuire, Colby Hill Landscaping Co. page 160: Brian Vanden Brink page 161: (BL) Jerry Pavia; (TR) Randall Perry; (BR) Walter Chandoha page 162: (T) Bill Rothschild; (B) Carolyn Bates, design and installation: Thomas Vanacore page 163: Tony Giammarino page 166: (T) Charles Mann; (B) Jerry Pavia page 168: (TL) John Glover; (BR) Carolyn Bates page 169: Bill Rothschild pages 170–171: Walter Chandoha pages 172: (TR), (C) Charles Mann; (B) Carolyn Bates, design and installation: Paul Wieczoreck, Champlain Valley Landscaping page 173: Charles Mann page 174: (T) John Glover; (B) Gay Bumgarner page 175: (T) Derek Fell; (B) Walter Chandoha page 176: (TR) Carolyn Bates, design and installation: Bill Henchey, Mansfield Lanscaping; (C), (BR) Michael S. Thompson page 177: Carolyn Bates, design and installation: Will Cunningham page 178: (T) Michael S. Thompson; (B) Jerry Pavia page 179: Garden Picture Library/Marie O'Hara page 180: (top row, left to right) Grant Heilman/Jane Grushow; Galen gates; Galen Gates (bottom row) Dembinsky Photo Associates/Richard Shiell; Susan Roth; D. Cavagnaro; John Glover page 181: (top row, left to right) John Glover; Photo Researchers/Norm Thomas; Photo Researchers/E.R. Degginger; (bottom row) John Glover; Positive Images/Margaret Hensel; John Glover; (R) Rob Cardillo pages 182–183: Brian Vanden Brink Photos/Todd Caverly page 184: Richard Felber page 185: (T) Tony Giammarino; (BL) Carolyn Bates, design and installation: Stony Mason; (BR) Tony Giammarino page 186: *both* Brian Vanden Brink page 187: Brian Vanden Brink page 189: (T) Tria Giovan; (B) Jerry Pavia page 190: Brian Vanden Brink page 191: (T) Brian Vanden Brink; (C) John Parsekian/CH page 192: Brian Vanden Brink page 193: (TL) Alan and Linda Detrick; (TR), (BR) Tony Giammarino; (BL) Betty Crowell page 195: Brian Vanden Brink page 196: (TL) John Parsekian/CH; (BR) Walter Chandoha; (LC) John Parsekian/CH page 197: (T) Tria Giovan; (B) Brian Vanden Brink pages 198–199: Brian Vanden Brink pages 200–201: (T) Jerry Pavia; (BR) Walter Chandoha; (BL) Carolyn Bates, design and installation: Paul Wieczoreck, Champlain Valley Landscaping pages 202–203: *both* Jerry Pavia page 204: (T), (C) John Parsekian/CH; (B) Brad Simmons page 205: Carolyn Bates, design and installation: Paul Wieczoreck, Champlain Valley Landscaping page 206: (TL) Jerry Pavia; (BR) Positive Images/Patricia Bruno page 207: (T) Garden Picture Library/Vaughan Fleming; (B) Tony Giammarino page 208: Charles Mann page 209: Carolyn Bates, design and installation: Matthew Furney, Firestone Landscaping pages 210–211: (C) Mark Samu; (TR) Jerry Pavia; (BL) Walter Chandoha page 212: Jessie Walker page 213: Positive Images/Karen Bussolini, design: Johnsen Landscape & Pools page 214: Michael S. Thompson